Co⋯⋯t
F⋯th

ANDREW KILLICK

First Edition 2017

ISBN 978-0-9955307-2-0

© **2017 H. Andrew Killick**

British Library Cataloguing-in-Publication Data
A catalogue record for this book is available from the British Library.

Published by Destinworld Publishing Ltd.
www.destinworld.com
info@destinworld.com

Cover design: Benjamin Lambert
Cover image by Jennifer Scaife

Contents

Preface

I T ALL STARTED IN MARCH 2014 with a conference in Durham entitled "Confidence in the Bible". Reporting back with some brief articles in the church magazine led to thinking about more and more areas where Christians lack confidence. In Britain our faith is often ignored, marginalised or ridiculed by the world in general; while in other countries the attacks can take a much more violent form. So how can we maintain our confidence? This book is written for the ordinary churchgoers who don't quite know what they believe, and for the agnostic outsiders who are prepared at the very least to re-examine the issues.

The book is divided into forty short chapters, each with reading passages and discussion questions at the end. It can be used by individuals or groups. Forty chapters will provide a convenient daily study in Lent; or the chapters can be read selectively and in any order.

My grateful thanks to many who helped with this project: to Matthew Falcus the publisher; to Andy Dale and Ben Lambert for the cartoons; to the person (I don't know who it was) who sent me an email with bloopers from church magazines, some of which provided captions for the cartoons; and to my wife Karen, Dr Lucy Falcus, the Rev John Lambert, Dr John Littlehailes, Professor Walter Moberly and Dr John Taylor for reading drafts of chapters and making many helpful suggestions.

Andrew Killick November 2016

1

Confidence in the Existence of God

HOW DO WE KNOW THAT God exists? "In the beginning God created the heavens and the earth." Those are the first words of the first book of the Bible, and they seem to be echoed in the first verse of John's Gospel, "In the beginning was the Word". The verb "was" is in an emphatic position in the Greek text: it implies "In the beginning the Word already existed".

So the Bible doesn't start by trying to prove to the reader that God exists. Nor does it pause later on to discuss the question. It just carries on with the story of God's acts in Old and New Testament times. But perhaps this is not surprising. If we could prove that God exists in some mathematical, logical, philosophical or other way, we would be greater than God – which we aren't.

Are we therefore floundering in the dark, hoping that God exists but fearing that the world is rudderless and meaningless? If we cannot be 100% sure, can we at least be confident beyond all reasonable doubt? And where does faith come in? Hebrews 11.6 says "Without faith it is impossible to please God, because anyone who comes to him must believe that he exists and that he rewards those who earnestly seek him". There is no point in going to the station if you don't believe that railways exist and that the train can transport you to London. Similarly, there is no point in praying to God and turning to him for help and guidance if you don't believe he exists.

Creation: If we look first at the world around us, it is almost certain that matter exists and that we ourselves exist. (It is *just* possible to say the whole world is an illusion and we are no more than ideas in the mind of some higher being; but most people would not waste time on this strange theory.) So we now have a problem. Either we must believe in a Creator God who made the universe, or we must believe in uncreated or self-created matter, which includes life and the ability of living things to replicate themselves. Which is more likely? Which is easier to believe? Christians believe in the Creator God: "By faith we understand that the universe was formed at God's command, so that what is seen was not made out of what was visible" (Hebrews 11.3). Faith is the only way we can be sure that God created the world out of nothing; but is it blind faith, or has faith got any substantial basis? We must approach the question from a different direction.

God's acts in the Old Testament: The subject of most of the Old Testament is the history of the Jewish nation. That story contains so many instances of what look like acts of God that it becomes very hard to attribute them all to coincidence and deny his existence. There are the major acts like the plagues of Egypt; the parting of the sea so that Israel could cross in safety but then the pursuing Egyptians were drowned; the pillars of cloud and fire that guided Israel by day and by night; the provision of food and water throughout the forty years of travelling in the desert; and the destruction of the walls of Jericho. There are also numerous less spectacular acts like giving Joseph the power to interpret dreams and so predict the seven years of famine; giving victory to Israel over the Amalekites, but only when Moses was holding up his hands in prayer; helping the young shepherd boy David to defeat the mighty warrior Goliath; answering Elijah's prayer for fire to consume the sacrifice when he was confronting the prophets of the false god Baal; and preserving Daniel when he was thrown into the lions' den, while his accusers when they were later thrown in were consumed even before they hit the floor.* Some have tried to explain away individual events as coincidences with natural explanations. But even then the timing of the events is remarkable, and cumulatively the evidence is strong that God was at work.

Jesus: In the Gospels we read of a man whose teaching and miracles were amazing, who was executed by professional Roman soldiers and yet was seen alive again by many witnesses a few days later, and who claimed to be one with the Father. He showed his divine power by turning water into wine, calming a storm and raising dead people. When a paralysed man was let down through the roof, Jesus first said his sins were forgiven (something that the onlookers knew only God could do) and then as proof of who he was he healed him.** Later New Testament writers declared "He [Jesus] is the image of the invisible God" and "In these last days he [God] has spoken to us by his Son…The Son is the radiance of God's glory and the exact representation of his being" (Colossians 1.15 and Hebrews 1.2-3). What do we make of all this?

The twelve disciple were slow to cotton on to who Jesus was. One of them said "Lord, show us the Father and that will be enough for us". Jesus answered "Don't you know me, Philip, even after I have been among you such a long time? Anyone who has seen me has seen the Father" (John 14.8-9). All the evidence points in one of three directions. Jesus was either mad, or bad, or God. He was either deluded, or playing a gigantic con trick which his disciples failed to see through for the next twenty centuries, or he was exactly who he claimed to be. We will look at the reliability of the Bible in the following chapters of this book; and if the evidence is found to be strong, we can be much more certain that God exists and that he has revealed himself in Jesus.

Later Christian experience: On the Day of Pentecost, ten days after Jesus had left his disciples and gone back to heaven, they were completely transformed. The Holy Spirit came down with a rushing wind, flames of fire, boldness and the gift of speaking in other languages. That is how Luke describes the events in Acts 2.1-41. The crowds in Jerusalem were amazed, and some were mocking and sceptical; but many were convinced and joined the group of believers. So was born the Church, and despite many periods of terrible persecution from Roman times right up to the present day, despite its own many failures and the infiltration of false teachers, the Church has survived and in several parts of the world is continuing to grow fast.

Every Christian since then has a story to tell. Some seem very ordinary, some are spectacular. Fred Lemon was a violent criminal in Dartmoor prison, but he was totally changed one night when three men in suits appeared in his cell and one of them, pointing to the figure in the middle, said "Fred, this is Jesus".*** Gram Seed's life had been messed up by football-related violence, robbery, assault, heavy drinking and drugs. He attempted suicide. He lived on a bench near Middlesbrough Post Office in all weathers, till a group of Christians told him that Jesus loved him. They later prayed for him as he spent six days in a coma. At the end of his time in hospital he knew something had changed: he became a Christian, and now leads a successful prison ministry organisation.****

For reading:
John 1.1-18; 1 John 1.1-4

For discussion:
a) Why were the disciples so slow to recognise who Jesus was?
b) What are the strongest arguments for the existence of God?
c) How can we present these arguments to our friends more effectively?

---

* These episodes can be found in Exodus 7-12; Exodus 14; Exodus 13.20-22; Exodus 15.22-16.18; Joshua 6.15-20; Genesis 41; Exodus 17.8-16; 1 Samuel 17; 1 Kings 18.30-40; Daniel 6

** John 2.1-11; Matthew 8.23-27; John 11.1-44; Mark 2.1-12

*** Fred Lemon with Gladys Knowlton: Breakout (Lakeland 1977) page 109-110

**** www.sowingseeds.org.uk/our-story

2

Confidence in the Bible (1) - transforming lives?

T HE GREAT 19TH CENTURY PREACHER Charles Spurgeon said "Defend the Bible? I would just as soon defend a lion." The Bible has a remarkable power and resilience that has defied all the attacks on it down the centuries and remains the world's best-selling book today. In the New Testament we read of people whose lives were changed by reading the Scriptures (which in those days meant the Old Testament). For example, when Paul came to Berea in northern Greece, "they received the message with great eagerness and examined the Scriptures every day to see if what Paul said was true. Many of the Jews believed…"(Acts 17.11-12). Then there was Timothy, to whom Paul wrote "Continue in what you have learned…from infancy you have known the holy Scriptures, which are able to make you wise for salvation through faith in Christ Jesus" (2 Timothy 3.14-15). Christians would say that the power of the Bible is due to God, the Divine Author speaking through the human writers.

In the 20th century the American preacher Billy Graham said that the more scripture he quoted in his addresses, the more people responded. There are many stories of people whose lives have been transformed by the Bible: here are just a few, with names changed to protect identities.

Amanda had a difficult, belligerent and rarely sober father. Even in hospital with incurable lung cancer he flippantly rejected her attempts to make him take God seriously, joking that God would never want to save a wastrel like him. But then he found a Gideon Bible by his hospital bed, started reading it, and on Amanda's next visit (a few days before his death) he was serious, subdued and in tears. She told him about God's love and Jesus' death on the cross, and that night he prayed for God's forgiveness.

Georgina was a 16 year old girl with severe mental health problems and no family support. After spells in rehabilitation hostels she was going to end her life by jumping under a tube train, but two policemen rescued her. Later, in an intensive care ward, pacing up and down in desperation, she tore open a locker, found a Bible, and held it tight as she prayed "Please, if there is a God, please, please, help me...". Immediately she found a feeling of peace and light and love which has not left her twenty years or more later.

David was given a Bible while in prison, came to faith, and wrote to the Gideons asking if a Bible could also be given to his girlfriend Megan. They had attended church as teenagers but then had given up going. However Megan had continued to pray for David, and as they studied the Bibles they had been given their lives got back on track - marriage, family, steady jobs and church involvement.

Kevin received a Gideon New Testament at school when he was 12, but it remained unopened in a blazer pocket and then in a drawer at home. Sixteen years later marriage and a young family prompted his wife to ask searching questions, and to find the answers at a local Chapel. Kevin too was asking questions, eaves-dropping on the Bible study group now being held in their home and starting to read that little New Testament. As a truck driver he had plenty of opportunities to read it while resting in a layby, and gradually he too came to faith.

Sue was another who received a New Testament at school but didn't read it till several years later. But at 21, facing questions about life, where we come from and whether there is a loving God, she spent three weeks reading the Bible and began to find the answers she needed.

Ben came from a church background. When he was aged 9 he wanted to be Christened, and he was given a Gideon Bible. His parents explained how to use it to look up passages when faced with particular situations and difficulties. Shortly after that an incident at school made him angry, but he remembered a passage he had read in the Bible about anger, and this helped him to remain calm.

A pastor from Myanmar who received a Bible from a Christian organisation said "For many years I have not had the Bible, because there are no Bibles in our place...This is the most precious gift I have ever received during my lifetime. I really love to read the Bible and I love to meditate on the word of God. It gives me light when I am in the dark".

Another pastor in the war-torn country of South Sudan said "I met a woman whose husband had been killed in the violence in 2013. She had been lonely and believed that God had killed her husband. She refused to go to church in protest but, one day as she was passing our office, she saw many people come in to buy Bibles. So, she decided to come in and buy one too, despite the fact that they cost more than a day's wage. As she's continued to read her Bible, her life has been changed. Now she says that her favourite verse is John 1.45 because she has discovered God".

A Bible Society worker in the refugee camp in Calais met a young Ethiopian and gave him a Bible. He said that Mark 10.27 was his favourite verse, "all things are possible with God". It had helped him through dark times: he had been in the camp five months, not wanting to be, but believing that God was showing him patience.

These stories have been taken from newsletters issued by the Barnabas Fund (Barnabasaid September/October 2015), the Bible Society (Word in Action Spring 2016) and the Gideons, an organisation dedicated to distributing Bibles in hotels, hospitals and elsewhere (Gideon News Autumn 2014 and Spring 2015). Similar stories can be found in churches and in the magazines of other Christian organisations. They mirror the experience described by some of the writers of the Bible. For example the writer of Psalm 119 said "Your word is a lamp to my feet and a light for my path" (Psalm 119.105), and Paul wrote to Timothy about the scriptures having been his guide from infancy, bringing him to faith and training him for Christian service (2 Timothy 3.14-16). In an age when the Church has had its confidence in the Bible dented, we need to uncage the lion.

For reading:
2 Timothy 3.10-17

For discussion:
a) What part if any has the Bible played in your life up till now?
b) What stories have you heard of people whose lives were affected by the Bible?
c) Why do you think the Bible changes lives?

3

Confidence in the Bible (2)
- an irrelevant book?

DESPITE THE STORIES IN THE previous chapter of lives being changed, the Bible and God and the Church are very much under attack at present. Atheists like Richard Dawkins (author of The God Delusion and other books which are hostile to Christianity) attack the idea of God's existence, and TV comedians like Ricky Gervais get plenty of laughs out of mocking Christians and Biblical stories. Members of the church and those who feel the Bible should be taken seriously can easily get discouraged. So how should we react to these attacks?

We could bury our heads in the sand - just carry on being church - irrelevant, out of touch. Or we could wring our hands - yes, it's so unfair, but what can we do? Or we could march around with long faces carrying placards with messages like "Prepare to meet your God". Or we could join the debate, do some hard thinking, listen, read some books, be polite, and earn the right to engage with our atheist friends. 1 Peter 3.15-16 encourages us always to be ready to give an answer to those who question us about our faith.

So what charges do the atheists bring against the Bible? Here are seven common ones, which we shall examine in the course of this chapter and the next. It's old. It's irrelevant. It's full of contradictions. It's unscientific. It's unbelievable. It's far too bloodthirsty in places. And why were those particular 66 books chosen anyway?

1. It is indeed old - a collection of 66 books by about 40 different authors writing between about 1200 BC and 100 AD. But age alone should not invalidate a book. We still read Greek plays from the 5th century BC (Aeschylus, Sophocles, Euripides, Aristophanes), or Greek philosophers from the 4th century BC (Plato and Aristotle), and find them valuable and full of important insights.

2. Is it irrelevant? For those who believe there is a Creator God, who made us and the whole universe and who desires a relationship with us, nothing can be more important than finding out what he is like and what he says and asks of us.

    For those who don't believe in such a God, there is still a lot of helpful advice on life, making the Bible far from irrelevant. "The love of money is a root of all kinds of evil... Do not store up for yourselves treasures on earth, where moth and rust destroy, and where thieves break in and steal...Who of you by worrying can add a single hour to his life?...Therefore do not worry about tomorrow, for tomorrow will worry about itself...The lips of an adulteress drip honey, but in the end she is bitter as gall...Wine is a mocker and beer a brawler; whoever is led astray by them is not wise...Train a child in the way he should go, and when he is old he will not turn from it...Do not boast about tomorrow, for you do not know what a day may bring forth...A fool gives full vent to his anger, but a wise man keeps himself under control...There is a time for everything, and a season for every activity under heaven: a time to be born and a time to die, a time to plant and a time to uproot...Carry each other's burdens...Keep your lives free from the love of money and be content with what you have...Do to others as you would have them do to you..." (1 Timothy 6.10; Matthew 6.19, 27, 34; Proverbs 5.3-4; Proverbs 20.1; Proverbs 22.6; Proverbs 27.1; Proverbs 29.11; Ecclesiastes 3.1-2; Galatians 6.2; Hebrews 13.5; Luke 6.31.). There's much wisdom here, whether or not we believe in God.

3.   I suspect that many people who claim the Bible is full of contradictions have barely opened its pages, or if they have, they cannot actually point out any contradictions. The eagle-eyed reader will spot the apparent discrepancy in consecutive chapters of 1 Samuel: in chapter 16.21-23 King Saul summons the young David to play music for him when he is unwell, yet in chapter 17.55-58 he doesn't know him and seems to be meeting him for the first time. But this could be imperfect editing of two different sources; or it could be memory loss caused by his illness, and courtiers who were wise enough not to point out the king's error. For a discussion of some seeming contradictions in the Gospels, see the chapter "Confidence in the Gospel Writers".

4.   People who say the Bible is contradicted by science are probably referring to Genesis and the account of creation in seven days. But does "day" in Genesis 1 mean a period of 24 hours? The repeated reference to evening and morning invites the reader to think in those terms, with a week of creation culminating in the seventh day as a day of rest. But we must think more about the type of writing this is - the literary genre. The whole chapter is more like poetry than a science textbook: see the discussion in the chapter "Confidence in Science". Poetry can convey truth, but it should not be read and interpreted in the same way as you would a historical or scientific textbook.

For reading:

John 6.66-69; 1 Peter 3.15-16

For discussion:

a) How do you answer the charge that the Bible is irrelevant?

b) How do you explain "the reason for the hope that you have" (1 Peter 3.15)?

c) What different views do people have of Genesis chapter 1 and Creation; and does it matter that these views are so diverse?

4

Confidence in the Bible (3) – an unbelievable book?

IN THE PREVIOUS CHAPTER WE listed seven common objections to the Bible, and we will now examine the final three.

5. Is the Bible unbelievable? Take miracles: many remarkable and miraculous events are recorded in its pages, particularly in the Gospels. But a miracle seems to break the physical laws of the world that we observe every day, so for some people it is an impossibility, and therefore they reject the Bible. However if God exists, if he created this world and the physical patterns within which it operates, it can hardly be doubted that he can override those "laws" when he chooses. We will examine the problem of miracles in chapter 8, "Confidence in Science".

So the problem of miracles disappears in the face of a much greater problem: can we believe in the existence of an invisible but all-powerful, miracle-working creator God? If we can, we shall not be able to fathom how he exists, but we shall be able to accept miracles. If we can't, we have the problem of how self-created matter can exist.

Rather than embarking upon a philosophical discussion, which is unlikely to reach a solution, we need to approach this dilemma from a different angle. We can start with Jesus: is there evidence that he lived, that he performed miracles, that he rose from the dead? That last event is stupendous and world-changing, *if* it happened. It means that we can rely on the God who is at work in the world and in human history, rather than relying on our own limited powers of reasoning. Now, there is evidence for Jesus as a historical figure not only in the Gospel writers (who might be accused of bias) but also in the Roman writers Suetonius, Tacitus and Pliny, and in the Jewish writer Josephus. These authors, born around the middle of the first century AD, were indifferent or hostile to Christianity, which makes their evidence all the more important and compelling. We will examine these issues in more depth in chapters 6 and 12, "Confidence in the Resurrection" and "Confidence in the Gospel Writers".

6. Is the Bible too bloodthirsty? Parts of the Old Testament in particular cause some people to describe God as evil, cruel, even a genocidal megalomaniac. In the face of such hostile criticism we need to look hard for responsible Christian ways of reading the tough passages. Why were the cities of Sodom and Gomorrah destroyed (Genesis 19.1-28)? Because of sin - not just some minor peccadillos but an ingrained lifestyle of violent sexual perversion. Why were the Egyptians destroyed in the Red Sea (Exodus 14.5-28)? Because Pharaoh hardened his heart: having allowed the Israelites to depart he changed his mind, and he refused to recognise the reality and power of the Lord (see Exodus 8.15, 19, 32). Why were the Amorites destroyed (Joshua 10)? Because they *chose* to oppose the Lord and his people. Why was Achan stoned to death after the capture of Jericho (Joshua 7.1-26)? Because he coveted some of the captured treasures and hid them in his tent, despite the leader's clear command to destroy everything. It is hard. But

sin has consequences. Opposing God has consequences. We must remember too that it is not up to us to say what happened to Achan or the Amorites or the Egyptians after death; we can only say with Abraham "Will not the judge of all the earth do right?" (Genesis 18.25) and leave the issue in God's hands.

7. Why are these particular books in the Bible, while others (maybe equally valuable or even better) are excluded? Isn't that bias? To answer these questions, we need to see how the two parts of the Bible came into being. The Old Testament was already in its present form by the first century AD. Jesus himself set his stamp of approval on it, by studying, fulfilling and underlining it. He studied it, and so was able to quote scripture at Satan when tempted in the wilderness (Luke 4.4, 8, 12); he was conscious of fulfilling its prophecies (for example Luke 4.16-21 and Luke 24.44); and he underlined its authority when he said in an aside "and the Scripture cannot be broken" (John 10.35). Paul too, referring to the Old Testament, asserted that all scripture is inspired by God (2 Timothy 3.16).

Can we make the same claims for the inspiration and authority of the New Testament, and how was the canon of its books chosen? (Canon is a Greek word meaning list.) Paul's letters had begun to be collected and regarded as authoritative by the time 2 Peter 3.15-16 was written, maybe around 63 AD (though the date is uncertain). The writer seems to have been aware of the need to preserve Christian documents now that the first generation of Church leaders was dying away (see 2 Peter 1.12-16). This process of collecting and approving continued until by the end of the 4th century AD the list of the 27 New Testament books was fixed. The various church councils didn't *choose* the books: rather, they set their seal of approval on books that were already widely accepted and had apostolic authority - that is, they had been written by one of the twelve Apostles or by people close to them. So it was the whole body of the Church, through its councils, that recognised the inspiration and authority of the Bible.

For reading:
2 Peter 1.12-21; 2 Peter 3.15-16

For discussion:
a) Old, irrelevant, full of contradictions, unscientific, unbelievable, bloodthirsty, too restrictive - which of those seven charges against the Bible do you hear most frequently?

b) How confident are you in answering them or any other attacks on the Bible?

c) Why do people find it so hard to believe in miracles?

5

Confidence in the Church

THE CHURCH OFTEN ATTRACTS NEGATIVE publicity. Totally irrelevant and out of touch, declining attendance figures (in the UK at least: the situation is quite the opposite in other parts of the world), homophobic, obsessed with what the world regards as unimportant issues like the role of women, saddled with obsolete buildings, tainted by scandals involving abuse or money...the list of charges is endless. And that is only in the present: there are also such causes of shame as the Inquisition, the selling of pardons and the internecine fighting between the Catholics and the Protestants in past centuries.

Worse still, some churchgoers in this country aren't even worried. One minister I know was talking with his elderly congregation about the need to make a few changes and to be more attractive to outsiders. But they wouldn't dream of it: they wanted things to remain exactly as they had always been. Wouldn't that mean that when they were gone that local church would just die? "Oh, we don't mind, because we won't be here!"

But what exactly is the Church? In the Apostles' Creed we find the phrases "I believe in the Holy Ghost; the Holy Catholic Church; the Communion of Saints...". Catholic means universal (not just Roman Catholic). So the Church does not consist of buildings but of all Christians down the ages, and today's believers in Jesus are linked in a common bond with their fellow believers whether they are alive today or have moved on to eternal rest on another shore and in a greater light.

C.S.Lewis makes this clear in an amusing way (see chapter 2 of *The Screwtape Letters*). Here is a senior devil berating a junior tempter for failing to halt his patient's move to faith: "One of our great allies at present is the Church itself. Do not misunderstand me. I do not mean the Church as we see her spread out through all time and space and rooted in eternity, terrible as an army with banners. That, I confess, is a spectacle which makes our boldest tempters uneasy. But fortunately it is quite invisible to these humans..." Screwtape expects that the actual buildings of the local church and its quirky congregation will be quite sufficient to put outsiders off. And he's probably right.

But the reality is very different. Jesus has built the Church on the foundation of Peter and the other apostles (Matt 16.18); he is the head of the Church (Colossians 1.18); and he loved the Church and sacrificed himself for her (Ephesians 5.25). We see a very imperfect Church, a band of flawed human beings, while God sees a Church clothed in Christ's perfection, dressed like a bride on her wedding day - the picture of the new Jerusalem found in Revelation 21.2.

Several consequences flow from these premises.

- We need to revise our mental picture of the Church. We need to support it rather than mock it, to value it as highly as God does, and to realise that we cannot grasp the full picture.
- We all have a part to play and different gifts to exercise in the local church - like the different parts of a human body (a picture Paul uses in 1 Corinthians 12.12-31).

- It is hard to be a Christian in isolation. Some people claim they can worship God just as well in the desert as in a church; and that may be true up to a point. But a burning log removed from the fire gradually stops burning and grows cold, yet it soon starts burning again and contributing to the fire when it is replaced.

- We need the support and encouragement of our fellow believers. Hebrews 10.25 says "Let us not give up meeting together, as some are in the habit of doing, but let us encourage one another". Sometimes we will be the ones needing encouragement, sometimes we will be able to offer it to others.

- While recognising that the Church is often scorned and mocked unfairly, we should not go out of our way to look ridiculous: we need to be as credible as possible. That will mean avoiding things like old-fashioned language, dirge-like hymns, and what you might call the seven deadly psins of preaching - being patronising, parsonical, pointless, pugnacious, pious, pompous or prayerless. Whoever aspires to preach the Gospel message or to teach believers has so many pitfalls to avoid...

Acts 2.42 gives us an ideal pattern for local church life: "They devoted themselves to the apostles' teaching and to the fellowship, to the breaking of bread and to prayer". These were new converts, and each of those four elements was important for them. When people first make a conscious decision to follow Jesus, there is so much still to learn. They need the help, guidance and encouragement that fellowship provides. The celebration of the Lord's Supper (or Holy Communion or the Breaking of Bread) is something Jesus has commanded his followers to do - see Luke 22.19. And our private praying will be complemented and strengthened by praying with others. So, whatever the world may think, the local church is very important after all.

For reading:
Acts 2.42-47; Ecclesiastes 4.9-12

For discussion:
a) What are the difficulties of trying to be a Christian in isolation?

b) Do we need to revise our view of what the Church is?

c) What are the most important things for the local church to do, and to avoid?

6

Confidence in the Resurrection
– A Conversation from
221B Baker Street

D <u>RAMATIS</u> <u>P</u>ERSONAE: Dr Watson (having just returned from his Club) and Mr Sherlock Holmes (lounging in his favourite armchair)

"Holmes! What do you make of this idea that's going round, that the resurrection of Jesus never happened?"

"Well, Watson, I confess that it's not my primary field of study. Nevertheless there do seem to be some parallels between solving a crime and solving the mystery of the vanishing body. So what's everyone saying?"

"Quite a few things, actually. But the basic claim is that miracles just simply can't happen. The resurrection if true would be a miracle. Therefore it never happened, QED."

"Very clearly put, Watson. And what is your opinion?"

"I don't know, Holmes. Sometimes I listen to the Gospel accounts and find them utterly convincing, and then I hear some well known speaker arguing that the whole idea is impossible and ridiculous. You've often said that when we have eliminated the impossible, whatever remains, however improbable, must be the truth. So what do you think happened, if resurrection is impossible?"

"Well, Watson, there are at least six different theories, and we need first to dig down to foundation level. Let me summarise them and then look at each one briefly:

1. Jesus never existed.
2. Jesus did exist, but the story of the crucifixion and resurrection is made up.
3. The body was stolen and hidden away by persons unknown.
4. Jesus didn't die on the cross; he revived in the coolness of the tomb and escaped.
5. The whole story doesn't matter very much anyway: it happened so long ago.
6. The Gospel writers are correct, and Jesus did rise from the dead."

"I can help you on that first point, Holmes. Quite apart from the Gospels, Jesus is mentioned by the Roman writers Tacitus, Pliny and Suetonius, none of whom would have had a bias in favour of Christianity. And that applies even more to the Jewish historian Josephus: I was reading his *Antiquities of the Jews* last week, and he has a long paragraph about Jesus. He's not friendly towards Christians, but it's good historical evidence."

"Quite so, Watson. I think no one nowadays can seriously believe that Jesus never lived. But if he did live, it is tempting to suggest that all those stories of resurrection and miracles are false - exaggerated, maybe, like that Chinese whispers game where the story grows each time someone passes it on. I can't believe that theory myself: the evidence is there in all those tiny little eye-witness touches. Take the account in John chapter 20. Peter and John run to the tomb; John, being younger, gets there first but is too shy to go in; then Peter arrives and barges straight in. It sounds so like the characters of the two men that we know from the rest of the Gospels! And again there's the curious incident of the burial cloth for his head lying separately and neatly folded. It all rings true! These are first-hand accounts. They were written by people who were actually there; and in those days there was much learning by heart and they had better memories than we have in our current educational climate."

"Yes, but could they have made up the story deliberately?"

"No, Watson, that really won't do. For a start, the Jewish authorities would have squashed the story by producing the body; but they didn't, because they couldn't. Secondly those early Christians were prepared to die for their beliefs in the following few years: they would never have done that if they knew that the whole story about the resurrection was a lie. And Paul talks about Jesus appearing after his resurrection to Peter, then to the Apostles, then to 500 at once, "most of whom are still living, though some have fallen asleep". That's what he says in 1 Corinthians 15, probably writing about 24 years after the event. So many witnesses - it adds up to a very convincing case that Jesus really did rise from the dead! Ah, is that Mrs Hudson I hear, coming up with the dinner? Let's take a short break."

* * * * *

"Right, Holmes, it's time to look at your next argument, and it's just the sort of thing Inspector Lestrade would say: "the body was stolen by persons unknown". Who had a motive for stealing the body?"

"It's not just motive, Watson. You also need to consider means and opportunity. There was a guard of soldiers at the tomb, and a massive stone over the entrance. So even if the disciples had a motive for stealing the body (which I don't think they did - they didn't want to base the rest of their lives on a lie), they didn't have the opportunity. The only people who had the authority to get past the soldiers were the Roman or Jewish leaders. But they had no motive: the Jews had set the guard in the first place, and they certainly didn't want rumours of a miraculous resurrection to circulate."

"So where have we got to? Theory number four is that Jesus never actually died, and just escaped from the tomb later."

"I hardly think so, Watson. Jesus must have been exhausted: no sleep for over 24 hours, the arrest and two trials during the night, the mockery, the crown of thorns and the flogging, the slow and painful journey out of the city stumbling as he tries to carry his own cross, the nails through his hands and feet, and then three hours or more of hanging on the cross and fighting for breath. The two criminals who were also crucified that day had to have their legs broken by the soldiers to hasten their deaths; but John records that the soldiers found Jesus was already dead - and Roman soldiers were professionals and would not have got that wrong. One of them pierced Jesus' side with a spear, and blood and water flowed out. John records this fact, even though at the time they didn't understand its significance."

"Holmes, I studied this during my training: it is good medical evidence for death - the separating of the red and white parts of the blood post mortem."

"Exactly so, Watson. So it is inconceivable that Jesus was still alive when he was buried - let alone the impossibility of escaping from the bandages, single-handedly shifting the heavy stone, slipping past the guards and looking remarkably alive over the next few days."

"Holmes, you see it all so clearly! I wish I had a brain like yours. But the fifth theory you listed was that it doesn't matter very much because it all happened so long ago."

"Ah, but it does matter! I might say that Julius Caesar never existed, or the Romans never built Hadrian's Wall. You might disagree, and we could have an entertaining argument about it. But if the resurrection actually happened, it is a world-changer. Human history can never be the same again. The eternal God has invaded our world of space and time, proved it by miracles including the resurrection, shown us a completely new way to live in the present, and conquered our ultimate fear - death. The clue is in the word eternal, Watson. It doesn't matter how many years ago it happened. It is still the most important event in history, and time cannot turn truth into a lie."

"Masterly, Holmes! So Jesus really did rise from the dead, and we can trust the Gospel accounts, with all those little eye-witness touches? Should we be worried about any contradictions between the four writers?"

"Look at the actual texts, Watson. One seeming contradiction is that Matthew mentions two women by name, Mark names three, Luke uses the plural women. Now, John only mentions one, Mary Magdalene; but then in chapter 20 verse 2 John records her as saying "They have taken the Lord out of the tomb, and we [not I] don't know where they have put him!" So there were several women at the tomb, and the Gospel accounts do harmonise: they are like four snapshots of the same event from different camera angles. And, Watson, there is one crowning argument we ought to mention. You have sometimes labelled me a misogynist in your stories of my cases - unfairly, I might say. But look at the place women have in this story. It was they who went to the tomb. They were the first witnesses to this extraordinary event. In first century Palestine (as in Greece and Rome) women were very much second class citizens compared with men; so if I had invented the whole story, I wouldn't have written it like that. And now, may we change QED to QEMDW? Quite elementary, my dear Watson!"

For reading:

The four accounts of the Resurrection can be read in Matthew 28.1-15, Mark 16.1-8, Luke 24.1-12 and John 20.1-18.

For discussion:

a) What difficulties are there in harmonising the four Gospel accounts of the Resurrection?

b) How would you answer critics who say Jesus didn't rise from the dead?

c) And how would you answer their claims that the whole story is unimportant and irrelevant?

7

Confidence in the Truth

IF WE TALK WITH PEOPLE about subjects like God, faith and truth, what do they usually say? "It may be true for you, but not for me - I believe in evolution", or "I tried praying once but it never worked". What exactly are they saying? Where can we discover the truth? Are all opinions equally true and equally valid? What is truth?

These are searching questions. Pontius Pilate was staring Truth in the face, yet he failed to recognise it. Scroll forward about 16 centuries to Francis Bacon (English statesman and philosopher, born 1561) who wrote, "*What is truth?* said jesting Pilate, and would not stay for an answer." Pilate's problem was that he just couldn't imagine the prisoner standing before him was anyone special.

Today we crave sound-bites and instant answers: like Pilate we haven't the patience to stay and listen and think. But if we did, there are at least three views on what truth is. There is relativism, there is pragmatism, and there is the correspondence view. It sounds complicated, but "bear with..." and all may become clearer!

People dismiss God with comments like "It may be true for you, but not for me: I believe in science, or evolution, or the Big Bang, or horoscopes, or blind chance, or living a decent life..." **This is relativism**; X may be true for you but not for me; truth depends on the person; truth is relative, not fixed.

Then there are the people who say "I tried praying once but it never worked." They want a God who proves that he's there, and the Christian God seems very remote, powerless and irrelevant. **This is pragmatism**; I'm a pragmatic person; X is only true when it works; prayer didn't work, so there is obviously no God out there to give me an answer.

But if I said "There is a radio in my kitchen" or "The Prime Minister of this country (at the time of writing) is Theresa May" or "Darlington is in the north east of England", these are statements that can be checked. They are either true or false, and by checking the facts we find that they do indeed correspond with reality. **This is the correspondence view of truth**; X is true because it agrees with factual reality.

The truth about the universe might be described as the sum total of all the statements that are true, the statements that correspond with the facts. There are thousands of unimportant facts, like my having had bread and jam for breakfast this morning; but we need to concentrate on the more significant facts.

Christians say that Jesus rose from the dead. What sort of statement is that? Is it true only for Christians? That's relativism. Is it true only for those who find it comforting and a help in their daily lives? That's pragmatism. Or did it really happen? Does it correspond with the facts? Can we say that the evidence backs it up and that it is true beyond all reasonable doubt?

It's as if we are in a lawcourt listening to the witnesses: we need to test their evidence and assess whether they are reliable. Evidence for the life, teaching, miracles, death and resurrection of Jesus Christ is certainly available. Here are three different strands of evidence: first the Gospels and Letters of the New Testament, second the Roman and Jewish writers like Tacitus and Josephus, and third the changed lives of Christians all over the world ever since. The sceptic may say that the New Testament writers are biased. But it is harder to dismiss the Roman and Jewish writers, who were no friends of the early Christians (see for example the sneering words of Tacitus *Annals* 15.44 and the slightly cynical tone of Josephus *Antiquities of the Jews* 18.3.3). As for the changed lives of Christians today, if they were only a few, they would be easy to dismiss; but it is difficult to ignore the millions who have found in Jesus Christ joy, forgiveness, confidence, healing, a certainty about the ultimate future, a new purpose in life in the present, and the willingness in some cases to endure horrendous suffering rather than deny their faith. So the claim that Jesus rose from the dead is backed up by good evidence.

But the word *truth* can also be used in a slightly different way. When Jesus said "I am the way and the truth and the life", he was claiming to be the most important truth in the universe, the embodiment of truth, one who was himself utterly truthful and reliable and who could lead his followers into truth. If we ignore him we are missing the ultimate reality, the foundation stone on which everything else is built.

For reading:

John 14.5-6; 1 John 5.20-21

For discussion:

a) Do you believe that truth is relative or absolute, and what do you understand by those terms?

b) What do you think Jesus meant when he said "I am the way and the truth and the life"?

c) To what extent do you accept, believe and live by Jesus' words?

8

Confidence in Science

HIS MAY SOUND LIKE A strange title! Surely everyone believes in Science nowadays, don't they? And Science has disproved the Bible, hasn't it? Ever since Darwin and the theory of evolution appeared in the 19th century, we know that Genesis is just a myth, don't we? Scientists know all the answers to life's questions; and if Genesis has got it all wrong, how can we believe in anything the Bible says?

But it's not quite that simple. Before Darwin there were scientists who were also believers. Kepler, for example, the great German astronomer (1571-1630), said he was "thinking God's thoughts after Him"; and over the entrance of the Cavendish Laboratory in Cambridge (opened in 1874) is a quotation from Psalm 111: "Great are the works of the Lord, sought out by all who have pleasure therein". The same is true today - there are many scientists on both sides of the debate, atheists and believers.

Let us examine three positions often held by atheists:

- They find it hard to take the Genesis account of creation seriously.
- They find it hard to accept miracles.

- Often they ignore the limitations of science: you hear them claim that even if we don't know the answer to a question now, we will one day.

Regarding Genesis, it is important to ask what kind of literature Genesis is. Is chapter 1 a song, a poem, history, satire, a letter, a science textbook? A telephone directory does not give advice on medical ethics or how to bake a cake; so if Genesis doesn't claim to be a science textbook, we are foolish to dismiss it as if it is. One highly respected astrophysicist (David Wilkinson, Principal of St John's College in Durham) suggests that chapter 1 is a hymn; for there are 7 Hebrew words in the first verse, 14 words in the second, and 21 mentions of God in the whole chapter (7 being a special number in Hebrew thinking). Note that days 1, 2 and 3 describe separating the shapeless, while days 4, 5 and 6 describe creating - filling the empty. It is also difficult to understand "days" as meaning periods of 24 hours, as the sun and moon don't appear till the fourth "day". This sounds much more like poetic language, and the people who mock Genesis for describing the creation of the world in six days fail to understand the literary genre. So the Bible tells us *that* God created the world, while science tells us a lot about *how*.

Regarding miracles, a 20th century German liberal theologian said "It is impossible to use electric light and the wireless and to avail ourselves of modern medical and surgical discoveries, and at the same time to believe in the New Testament world of Spirits and miracles".* He was saying that modern "miracles" (in inverted commas) have scientific explanations, so we can assume that first century "miracles" did too – they just didn't know what those explanations were.

The trouble with miracles is that they break the laws of physics. But these laws are provisional! All science is a collection of theories trying to explain what we see happening around us. Take Newton's Law of Gravity. When he saw the apple fall, he came up with his theory (gravity being derived from a Latin word meaning heaviness). Then along came other pieces of evidence suggesting that the earth and the apple both have a mass and therefore exert a pull on other objects: in this case the earth wins because it has a greater mass. So the earlier theory had to be revised, and the laws of physics are only the best explanations we have come up with so far: they are descriptive, not prescriptive. They cannot rule out unusual events which contradict the theories we have formed so far and which may in fact be special ("miraculous") acts of God.

Science has a duty to look at evidence. *Is* there evidence that people are healed in answer to prayer...that locked prison doors sometimes open "miraculously"...that Jesus really did rise again after the crucifixion and was seen by many witnesses? Yes, there is, if we are prepared to look at it with an open mind.* We mustn't hold on to the prejudice that science rules out miracles.

Regarding the limitations of science, scientists need to admit that they don't know all the answers. For example, what is light? Is it a wave, or a particle, or can it be both? Since the 1920s the evidence has pointed in two contradictory directions. Or, what are the implications of chaos theory, which came to prominence in the 1960s? Atoms don't always behave exactly as we think they will. What we thought was a mechanistic universe doesn't always keep what we thought were the rules, and the future has a degree of unpredictability about it. So scientists need to be more humble in their claims.

But Christians too sometimes need to be more humble and admit they don't know all the answers. How can God be three and yet one? How can he create a universe out of nothing? The text says simply "And God said, Let there be light, and there was light", and a bit later "He also made the stars" (Genesis 1.3, 16).

The former American President Roosevelt used to go outside at night and gaze at the stars and the vastness of the universe, which he saw as a good way of keeping humble.

Summing up, I believe in Science: scientists are *generally* doing a brilliant job in discovering more about the universe. I also believe in God and in the Bible as his word, his revelation to humanity. There are mysteries on both sides, and dialogue is needed rather than ears that are deaf to the arguments of others.

For reading:
Genesis 1.1; Psalm 19.1-6; Job 38.1-41

For discussion:
a) What are the three passages above saying, and what kind of literature are they?
b) Why is there such a conflict between religion and science?
c) How can that conflict be resolved?

---

* (R.Bultmann "New Testament and Mythology in Kerygma and Myth: a Theological Debate", ed. H.W.Bartsch, trans. R.H.Fuller, New York, Harper and Row 1961, page 5).

** For prison doors opening see Acts 12.1-19, Acts 16.22-28 and the remarkable story of Brother Yun's release from detention in China: "The Heavenly Man" by Brother Yun with Paul Hattaway, Monarch Books 2002, pages 62-68.

9

Confidence in the
Gospel Message

WHAT IS THE GOSPEL? How do we explain to someone exactly what it is and how we can become a Christian? Several years ago a vicar was being interviewed on local radio. He was asked two direct questions: how can we become a Christian, and what would you say to someone gravely ill in hospital with only a few days to live? He waffled. He seemed to have no clear message. His answer to both questions was on the lines of "Well, it takes a long time; you have to attend church regularly before you can understand". And there was I thinking - what a lost opportunity! How can anyone close to death attend church for several years to find out the answer to life's most important question?

When Jesus first started preaching and teaching, his message, as recorded in Matthew 4.17 and Mark 1.15 was "Repent, for the kingdom of heaven is at hand". John the Baptist had used the same message as he paved the way for Jesus' coming (Matthew 3.2); and Peter used similar words in his first two sermons in the book of Acts: "Repent, and be baptised every one of you in the name of Jesus Christ for the forgiveness of your sins" and "Repent therefore, and turn again, that your sins may be blotted out" (Acts 2.38 and 3.19 RSV). It's a simple message.

The word gospel literally means good news. But first there is the bad news: our sinfulness. We need to repent – which means saying sorry for the wrong things we have done, turning away from them and starting to go in a different direction in life. Those who think they are living pretty decent lives on the whole and don't need forgiveness from God will switch off at this point, because they don't grasp the bad news. They will not be excited by the good news - that God loves us in spite of everything we have done, that he sent Jesus to die on the cross and so take the punishment we deserved, and that he is longing to forgive us when we turn back to him.

So how do we repent? We need to talk to God in prayer. Prayer can be silent in our minds or spoken out loud; it can be in church or at home or walking in the country or anywhere you like; it can be your own words or a more formal prayer written by someone else - all that's needed is that you should really mean the words. It might go like this:

"God, I am sorry for all the wrong things I have said and done and thought. Thank you for loving me and sending Jesus to die on the cross in my place. Please come into my life and help me to live in a way that pleases you from now on."

And what happens then? If we meant what we said, it is like opening a door. "Here I am! I stand at the door and knock. If anyone hears my voice and opens the door, I will come in and eat with them, and they with me." These are the words of Jesus in a letter to a church full of luke-warm believers (Revelation 3.20 TNIV). It is a verse that really helped me (good solid Church of England, confirmed at school and trying to read the Bible and pray) actually to become a Christian. And he promises that he *will* come in - not he *might*, or he *will subject to a trial period of six months*. It is a definite promise, with life-changing consequences!

Jesus brings pardon...peace...a new purpose to our existence... power to live a better life...and his presence constantly with us. For one of my friends, who became a Christian at university, it meant an end to loneliness. For some it will also mean healing, as it did when Peter preached those first two sermons in Acts 2 and 3. We will *want* to read the Bible, to pray, to meet with our fellow believers for teaching and encouragement, and to talk to others about our new-found faith. It all starts with one simple prayer.

For reading:

Acts 2.37-42; Revelation 3.14-22

For discussion:

a) What is the gospel?
b) Share with the group your own experience of encountering the gospel message.
c) How can we best explain that message to others?

10

Confidence in God's Forgiveness

I LOVE WATCHING COURTROOM DRAMAS ON television. There is that moment of suspense as the foreman of the jury is about to answer the question "Do you find the prisoner guilty or not guilty?" And then there is either a hush or an emotional outburst when the single word "Guilty" is spoken.

What is guilt? Here are four examples:

- Scenario 1: If I say harsh words to a loved one in the heat of the moment, I feel guilty and regret it afterwards.
- Scenario 2: If I drive at 40 mph along the High Street and then see the flashing lights of a police car behind me, I kick myself for being stupid.
- Scenario 3: If I make an illegal copy of a CD, I am breaking the law but I probably don't give it a second thought.
- Scenario 4: A neighbour invites me to a meal and I make the excuse that I am rather tired; and then I feel bad because they seem to ignore me thereafter and the opportunity to share a meal and friendship never returns. What is the difference (if there is any) between guilt and regret?

Regret is a human emotion, while guilt is a matter of fact - we have broken a law. In scenario 1 I have broken God's law "Love your neighbour as yourself". In scenario 2 I have broken the law of the land. So in both cases there is guilt AND regret. In scenario 3 I have broken the copyright law, so there is guilt even if there is no regret. In 4 there is no law that you must accept dinner invitations, and maybe there was an element of truth in my tiredness excuse; so there is regret, but no guilt.

How then do we deal with guilt, and how do we deal with regret? Both are important, but guilt is easier to deal with than regret - which may or may not seem surprising. If we have broken the law of the land, we need to be honest about it and make restitution and/or take the punishment: it is simple, but painful! If we have broken God's law (which we all have, because all humans are sinful and need God's forgiveness), we need to be honest with God and confess our wrong thoughts, words and deeds and the good things we knowingly failed to do: so again it is simple, but humbling.

And that is where the problems lie. Can it really be that simple? And am I prepared to swallow my pride? Some people think they are so bad that God cannot possibly forgive them - and nothing anyone says to them convinces them otherwise. But it is God himself who promises forgiveness! "If we confess our sins, he is faithful and just and will forgive us our sins and purify us from all unrighteousness" (1 John1.9). "Whoever comes to me I will never drive away" (John 6.37). "Ask and it will be given to you; seek and you will find" (Matthew 7.7). "Therefore, there is now no condemnation for those who are in Christ Jesus" (Romans 8.1). These are such clear promises, and similar promises occur in many other passages in the Bible. He WILL forgive...you WILL find...there is NO condemnation. All we need to do is come to God (by talking to him in prayer), say sorry (and mean it) and then trust in his promises.

Maybe that famous old hymn "There is a green hill far away" will help:

> He died that we might be forgiven,
> he died to make us good,
> that we might go at last to heaven,
> saved by his precious blood.
> There was no other good enough
> to pay the price of sin;
> He only could unlock the gate
> of heaven, and let us in.

Jesus died for us on the cross, he died in our place, and so he can take away our guilt. All we have to do is turn to him and confess our sins. Are we prepared to be humble enough - to admit that we have gone the wrong way in life and cannot put things right by our own strength or wisdom?

But how can we deal with regret? If we do take that first step of asking for God's forgiveness, are we then prepared to forgive ourselves? It's hard to "love our neighbour *as ourselves*" (a little phrase that we may not have noticed before). Yet if we don't take this second step, we shall have freedom from guilt but still carry the burden of regret. That's like being given a birthday cake but never actually eating it, or paying a cheque into our bank account but then never drawing out any money to use. Jesus has unlocked the gate of heaven, so if we have received his forgiveness, there's no point in not forgiving ourselves too.

For reading:

1 John 1.5-10

For discussion:

a) How easy do we find it to accept God's forgiveness?
b) How easy do we find it to forgive ourselves?
c) How can we best explain the terms darkness, light, sin, guilt and forgiveness to others?

11

Confidence in Old Age

SHAKESPEARE AND KING SOLOMON BOTH paint a depressing picture of old age. "Last scene of all, that ends this strange eventful history, is second childishness, and mere oblivion, sans teeth, sans eyes, sans taste, sans everything" (from the speech about the seven ages of man, in *As You Like It* act 2 scene 7). Solomon too (or whoever was the author of the book Ecclesiastes) contrasts youth and old age and seems to be referring to the failing of the teeth and the eyes: he writes (Ecclesiastes 12.1-5) "before the days of trouble come and the years approach when you will say, "I find no pleasure in them"... when the grinders cease because they are few, and those looking through the windows grow dim...when men are afraid of heights and of dangers in the streets...". Is old age some ghastly mistake or a phase of life to be dreaded?

In general the Bible is very positive towards old age. "Is not wisdom found among the aged? Does not long life bring understanding?" (Job 12.12). "The glory of young men is their strength, grey hair the splendour of the old" (Proverbs 20.29). "Your old men will dream dreams, your young men will see visions" (Joel 2.28). These passages suggest that all of God's people should be respected, all have a role in the work of building the Kingdom of God, and the old can offer the wisdom of experience to the young. Even more striking is a passage from Isaiah 46.3-4 which I only noticed recently; "Listen to me, O house of Jacob, all you who remain of the house of Israel, you whom I have upheld since you were conceived, and have carried since your birth. Even to your old age and grey hairs I am he, I am he who will sustain you. I have made you and I will carry you, I will sustain you and I will rescue you." Here there is no small print, or terms and conditions: God does not give up loving and sustaining people after a certain age.

So the writer of Ecclesiastes may well strike a chord with some, especially with those who have no awareness of a Heavenly Father who cares for them every step of the way. But he is writing after a lifetime of seeking pleasure through such things as work, wine, women and wealth; and these are things which ultimately lead to dissatisfaction and a sense of emptiness unless we take note of his injunction "Remember your Creator" (Ecclesiastes 12.1).

Faced with such perceived evils as illness, disability, dementia, and the consciousness of approaching death, we could despair, or we could bury our heads in the sand, or we could turn to God's word as the only source of truth and comfort. King Hezekiah was ill and close to death; but he prayed, he recovered, and afterwards he said "Surely it was for my benefit that I suffered such anguish" (see Isaiah chapter 38, especially verse 17). Paul wrote about the trials and temptations that come our way and asserted that "God is faithful; he will not let you be tempted beyond what you can bear" (1 Corinthians 10.13). Psalm 23.4 provides the most comforting reassurance in the face of the ultimate enemy: "Even though I walk through the valley of the shadow of death, I will fear no evil, for you are with me; your rod and your staff, they comfort me". We are not pretending that it is easy to face up to these things, or to care for those who are going through them; but we are saying that the presence and sustaining help of God makes all the difference, and that nothing is outside his knowledge and control.

So we should not dread old age. We should not feel we no longer have anything to contribute. We should not "retire" from active Christian service. We should never underestimate the contribution of those who, through force of circumstances, can "only" pray: they are probably doing the most important task. And churches work best when they have a mix of all ages and value every member of the body. Recently I spoke with an older man who had lost two wives through illness, but who was still trusting the Lord and saying "What does God want me to do with the rest of my life?"

For reading:
Ecclesiastes chapter 12.1-14; Psalm 23.1-6; Isaiah 38.1-22

For discussion:
a) How good are our local churches at looking after and valuing older people?

b) What have Christians to say in an age where assisted suicide is increasingly accepted, welcomed and used?

c) Is it realistic to say that Christians never retire?

EIGHT NEW CHOIR ROBES ARE CURRENTLY NEEDED
DUE TO THE ADDITION OF SEVERAL NEW MEMBERS
AND TO THE DETERIORATION OF SOME OLDER ONES

12

Confidence in the Gospel Writers – Another Conversation from 221B Baker Street

THERE WAS A HEAVY SIGH from the depths of Watson's armchair. Holmes, laconic as ever, said nothing. Another sigh, and then at last Watson gave voice to his concerns.

"I'm fed up, Holmes. The Club atheist has been holding forth again, saying that we can't trust the Gospel writers."

Holmes remained silent. It was only by the slightest raising of an eyebrow that anyone could tell he was listening.

"Well, say something, Holmes! Can't you give me at least something with which to counter his arguments?"

"My dear Watson, you know that I never theorise without data. There are probably a hundred ways by which you could attack the Gospel writers, and a hundred ways by which you could defend them. Give me some more information!"

"All right then. He has been saying that the Gospels are full of contradictions and inaccuracies. So he thinks the whole thing is one giant hoax, a conspiracy to make us believe certain things about a character from first century AD Palestine who never even existed. Or at the very least he wasn't what he claimed to be, the Messiah, the Christ, the Son of God. He was just a con artist."

"Did he give examples, to prove his point?"

"Yes. Take the Christmas story. There are no shepherds at the manger in Matthew, and no kings or Magi in Luke, while Mark and John leave out the story of the birth altogether! Then there's the so-called Lord's Prayer, so much shorter in Luke than in Matthew; and the Beatitudes are totally different - you know, that passage saying blessed are this lot and blessed are that lot. So is the story of feeding the five thousand - or four thousand in another version. He is pretty cynical about miracles in general, but even more cynical when they can't agree on the details. What about the confusions in the Easter story - what time in the morning was it, and how many women actually went to the tomb? As for the ending of Mark's Gospel, or should we say endings plural, it's a complete mess, and we haven't the foggiest idea what Mark actually wrote."

"Thank you, Watson. That gives us plenty to digest. Contradictions, inaccuracies, a hoax - these are all serious charges and deserve serious answers. Let us first remind ourselves that *if* (and for some it is a big *if*) the Gospels are honest historical accounts, they are written by human beings with all their human limitations. (They were also copied by hand and later translated by human beings with human limitations - but that's a topic for another evening's discussion.) The four Gospels often overlap, covering the same or similar incidents or parables; but the wording may differ slightly, and one writer may include a few extra details. There is certainly a deep underlying unity and harmony between them; but they are not constantly looking over their shoulders saying "I must check Matthew's exact wording for this story". Books were so much rarer and more cumbersome in those days - scrolls, without the convenience of page numbers.

"So they are very different. Mark's account is brief, pithy and action-packed: for example, have you noticed that he uses the word "immediately" or "at once" no less than eleven times just in chapter 1? Maybe he didn't feel the need to record details of Jesus' birth, because for him it was the life and teaching that were so much more important. Or maybe he just lacked sources of information for those early days. Matthew refers to many Old Testament prophecies fulfilled in Jesus' life. He seems to have been addressing Jews in particular, and he must also have had sources of information about the visit of the Magi. Luke was a Gentile, the only one of the four who was not a Jew. He had a historian's eye for accuracy, and he must have had conversations with Mary or people close to her, as he records so much about her thought-processes, for example when the angel first came to her. John was more reflective and philosophical: he puts a special emphasis on the "I am" sayings of Jesus, and on the "signs" (like turning water into wine) that demonstrated his divine power and glory. He too omits the Bethlehem story, but don't you think he sees deeper into the true significance of it - the light of the world coming down to live among humans?"

"Holmes, I knew I could rely on you. That goes a long way towards clearing up my difficulties about the story of the birth. But what about the different versions of the Lord's Prayer and the Beatitudes?"

"Well, Watson, how many times do you think Jesus talked about prayer, or about who is truly blessed? It would be astonishing if he always used exactly the same words each time. The writers may well be recording versions delivered on different occasions."

"And what about the miracles, and that confusion over numbers when he provided bread for the crowds?"

"People often fail to notice the simplest things, Watson. Read Matthew 16.5-11, where Jesus is talking about not one but two instances of feeding large crowds, and rebuking them for not learning lessons about his divine power even when they had seen the miracle performed twice! Why should such an event *not* have occurred twice? Honestly, Watson, critics of the Gospels can sometimes be so arrogant in the presumptions they make."

"But what about miracles in general? Some people make this a starting point in their thinking, that miracles simply cannot happen."

"Yes, Watson, we talked about this before when discussing the resurrection. You know my dictum: when you have eliminated the impossible, whatever remains however improbable must be the truth - if, that is, there is only one theory left. Well, last week we eliminated several alternative theories explaining away Jesus' rising from the dead, and it is unwise and illogical to dismiss the only theory that is still standing on the dubious grounds that it breaks the so-called laws of physics. After all, if God can create a universe out of nothing...Yes yes, I know your atheist friend would snort at that word *if*. But there were so many eye-witnesses to many of the miracles, and to the resurrection in particular. Paul talks about five hundred of them in 1 Corinthians 15.6, where he says that most of them are still alive as he writes that letter in the early 50s AD. Incidentally, it is highly probable that the Gospels and the Letters were written within a few decades of the events, when memories were still fresh and people could have stepped forward and corrected any errors."

"You are right, Holmes. And since our last discussion I have been reading the four accounts of the resurrection again and trying to bring some harmony into them - who exactly was there, what time it was and so on. You *can* make them fit together, as we said. And I guess that John had special information from Mary Magdalene that enabled him to give extra details."

"Well done, Watson. Here's another seeming contradiction that disappears on closer inspection. All four writers describe the hours leading up to the crucifixion and death of Jesus at considerable length; yet the famous "seven last words" are variously recorded. Matthew and Mark have just one (the quotation from Psalm 22.1 "My God, my God, why have you forsaken me?" - Matthew 27.46 and Mark 15.34), while Luke has three other sayings and John has yet another three that are not recorded in any of the other Gospels. Now, you know my methods, Watson. Should we be worried?"

"Holmes, I begin to see dimly what you are getting at. It's like your cases, where different witnesses each supply different parts of the jigsaw puzzle. We can see afterwards that they weren't contradicting each other, but each spoke from their limited knowledge, or the things they felt were the most important."

"I like that picture of the jigsaw puzzle, Watson. My own explanation would be on the lines of different photographs taken from various angles or at various times. But your illustration is just as good, and we reach the conclusion that you can usually find answers for people who say the Bible is full of contradictions."

"I did notice the confusion at the end of Mark's Gospel, suddenly breaking off almost in mid sentence and then having some extra bits added on. It looks as if later writers wanted to round things off. But why?"

"We can't be certain, Watson. As so often happens, there are probably a dozen good explanations. Here's one, and I must confess I think it is the most likely. Most people agree that Mark's Gospel was the first of the four to be written. Then Matthew and Luke both used Mark as a source and surpassed him in popularity, so Mark's Gospel was rather neglected. Anyway those early Christians probably didn't see the urgency of writing it all down: they may have thought that Jesus would soon be returning. When the years rolled on and the first generation of believers, all those eye-witnesses, began to die off, they realised it was important to collect all the written records they could find. Peter hints at this in one of his letters, and he mentions a collection of Paul's letters that were collected and regarded as important and authoritative. As they searched, they found just one copy of Mark; but it was battered and old, and the last few columns of the scroll had dropped off. So various people then or later on tried to round it off by adding some extra verses: you can see that they are in a different style and don't quite fit with the previous paragraph."

"Very interesting, Holmes. I think you may have hit the nail on the head. But we still haven't discussed the hoax theory. Couldn't the whole of the New Testament be a gigantic con trick?"

"There are at least five arguments against that theory, Watson, and all are in my view persuasive. Firstly, there are all those eye-witnesses who were still alive when the Gospels and the Letters were written. *Someone* would have kicked up a fuss if it was all untrue; or if you say all five hundred or more were in on the conspiracy, that is psychologically most unlikely. Secondly, what motive did they have to cover up a lie, especially when some of them had to give up their lives for that lie? Stephen was martyred, Peter and John were put on trial and beaten, Paul had a list as long as your arm of all the beatings, imprisonments and shipwrecks that he endured. And for what? For something they knew was untrue? No, Watson, that makes no sense. Thirdly, the Gospels sound like eye-witness accounts: they have the ring of truth. It's not something you can easily quantify; it's just the feel of them. Fourthly, if it really was a conspiracy, it could have been done so much more convincingly. They could have cut out those seeming discrepancies in the resurrection narratives, and they wouldn't have thought of women as being the first witnesses to the resurrection: women were very much second class citizens in those days. (No, Watson, that is a well known fact, it is not

Holmes the alleged misogynist speaking: sometimes I detect a little prejudice against me in those stories of yours!) But finally, have you read my monograph on Luke? Such a careful writer - a real historian. You will find a copy on the top shelf of the bookcase behind you; however we had better postpone a discussion about him till another time."

"Holmes, you are a genius! So you are 100% sure that the Gospels are true and reliable?"

"No, Watson - just 99.9% sure. I'm not like one of those uncritical folk who say it's just a matter of faith - you have to *believe* the Bible is reliable. We *do* need faith, but it is not blind faith: we have the facts and evidence on which to base our faith. What is it Inspector Lestrade is always saying? Not "proven beyond all doubt", but "proven beyond all *reasonable* doubt." If your club atheist won't listen to reasoned arguments, you will have to try a totally different approach. Take him to a concert; play a round of golf with him - anything that will win his friendship on more neutral ground and reassure him you are not some religious nutter..."

For reading:
John 20.30-31; John 21.20-25

For discussion:
a) What are the strongest arguments for not trusting the Gospel writers?

b) What makes you confident that Matthew, Mark, Luke and John are reliable?

c) How easy is it to trust the Gospel stories of miracles and healings?

13

Confidence in God's Guidance

HERE WAS A YOUNG COUPLE, John and Kathie, with a 2-year-old toddler and another baby on the way. He was getting on well in his career, and they were both involved in their local church. Then they were both struck by a passage in their daily Bible readings about taking the Christian message to the nations (Matthew 28.16-20). They told no one. A couple of weeks later a speaker at a carol service felt led to go off script: holding a lighted candle, he talked about the importance of taking the light to the nations, and said he felt sure God was calling someone present to take the light of Christ out into a dark place – perhaps where the name of Jesus was not known. A lady who was a friend of the couple instantly knew that this was a word for them. So they talked to the church leaders, who advised them that they needed to be trained first and then sent out. They started at a Bible College, though they wondered how all the fees and regular household expenses could possibly be met out of their non-existent savings. They needn't have worried: thanks to a large gift from their church as well as smaller gifts from friends, they found in the first month that they had exactly what they needed to cover their budget. Where would they go? At a service in the college the speaker talked about how the church was growing strongly in so many parts of the world, but not in Western Europe; and John and Kathie felt this was a call to France, despite their lack of confidence in foreign languages. Seventeen years later, after ordination and a fruitful ministry in several churches in Paris, they were wondering about moving on to a different part of the mission field – perhaps Spain. But none of the adverts in the Church of England Newspaper stood out for them, and then over the page was an advert for a post as Associate Minister in a church in the north of England. John just knew this was where they were being called to go. There were four others interested in the post, and John had a sudden and virulent stomach bug when he went for interview; but he was appointed. As it turned out, one of the interviewers felt this was a spiritual attack and a sure sign that he was the right candidate. One of the delightful little confirmatory signs since then has been a young French lady coming for baptism in the church and finding a minister who is fluent her language: he translated her words of testimony before the baptism, and then used the words "Je te baptise au nom du Père et du Fils et du Saint-Esprit". This is a story of God guiding step by step through the Bible, through friends, through church leaders, through Christian literature and even through illness. It is a story of God providing, and of confirming the choices they have made thus far.

Psalm 25 has much to say about God's guidance. It starts with focusing on the Lord (verse 1) and trusting in him (2), then moves on to praying to be shown his ways (4). The middle section (8-15) affirms that God does guide: "He guides the humble in what is right and teaches them his way…The Lord confides in those who fear him…My eyes are ever on the Lord, for only he will release my feet from the snare" (verses 9,14,15). An important condition for receiving guidance is that we should be humble, trusting and looking towards the Lord.

Some people hesitate to make a choice for fear of getting it wrong, but verse 12 might help them: "Who are they that fear the Lord? He will teach them the way that they should choose" (Psalm 25.12 NRSV). This verse implies that we don't sit back with a blank mind, waiting for inspiration: we have to do the fearing (that is, honouring God) and the choosing, while he does the instructing. We must choose, and he will guide. And if, with the best will in the world, we make a less good choice, God is great enough to understand, forgive and gently correct us.

Sometimes in the New Testament guidance came to a group. The church at Antioch were worshipping and fasting when the Holy Spirit spoke about sending out Barnabas and Saul on what was going to be the first of several missionary journeys (Acts 13.2-3). We don't know exactly how the Spirit spoke – whether audibly, or in the minds of one or more of the disciples gathered there, or in some other way. But it was clearly the right way forward, and the guidance was given while they were praying and focusing on God.

So what are the ways in which God guides? Here, in no special order, are some of the ways:

A passage of the Bible can sometimes leap off the page: having read it we are utterly certain that this applies to us in our own situation.

Friends often know us better than we know ourselves; and if they say something like "You would be ideal for that task", we may well sit up and take notice.

Church leaders can have a similar role in prompting us, or in refining ideas we have already begun to think through.

Our conscience is sometimes stirred: we hear of some need and realise that we cannot ignore it. A minister in a church in the north east of England was walking up the High Street of a neighbouring town, praying that the Lord would send a new minister to the struggling church there; and then he received the very clear answer "It's you!"

An inner conviction can come suddenly or gradually. Maybe we are weighing up two courses of action, listing the pros and cons of each and slowly finding the balance swinging in one direction: we feel a growing sense of unease, or an inner peace, about one of our options.

Circumstances can of themselves be a powerful guiding light. Some doors close, while others open. Someone once said "There is no point in trying to make a final decision about a job until the post is actually offered to you".

Our gifts – the things we are good at – can be an indication of where we should get involved. We enjoy chatting with new people, or playing sport, or cooking; so start a new book club, join the cricket team, or offer to help with the church lunch club.

A prophetic word is sometimes given, maybe in the context of a church service or a Bible study group. It may be addressed directly to us, or it may be announced in the meeting and we realise that it's a message for us.

Dreams came to Joseph and to the Wise Men at important moments in the story of Jesus' birth; and today God still uses this means of communication at times.

Most of these forms of guidance come into play at decision-making times, when we arrive at the various cross-roads in life – university course, job, marriage, which church to attend, responsibilities within the church, leisure interests, educating children, moving house and so on. But a lot of guidance is more general and common to all Christians (like our DNA makeup, which is 99% or more shared by all humans). Should we read the Bible, pray, attend church, eat, sleep, get up in the morning (if we are not ill or working at night), use money wisely, control our tempers? Reading the Bible can educate our consciences and be our memory bank in the 1001 little decisions of each day. Paul says to Timothy (2 Timothy 3.15) "From infancy you have known the holy scriptures, which are able to make you wise for salvation through faith in Christ Jesus".

For reading:
Acts 16.6-10

For discussion:
a) What factors were at work in the way Paul and his companions found the way ahead in Acts 16?

b) What do you think are the most important conditions for receiving God's guidance?

c) In what ways have you experienced God's guidance in the past?

14

Confidence in Worship

"**S**HOUT FOR JOY TO THE Lord, all the earth. Worship the Lord with gladness; come before him with joyful songs...Enter his gates with thanksgiving and his courts with praise; give thanks to him and praise his name" (Psalm 100.1-4). So many of the psalms, especially around Psalm 100, invite us to sing and praise God.

Psalm 95 (sung down the centuries as the Venite in the Church of England's Morning Prayer) says "Come, let us sing for joy to the Lord; let us shout aloud to the Rock of our salvation. Let us come before him with thanksgiving and extol him with music and song...Come, let us bow down in worship, let us kneel before the Lord our Maker". The psalm reminds us that he created the world, that we are his people, and that we need to listen to his voice.

Psalm 96 says "Sing to the Lord a new song; sing to the Lord, all the earth. Sing to the Lord, praise his name; proclaim his salvation day after day...For great is the Lord and most worthy of praise; he is to be feared above all gods." This psalm calls on us to give him due glory, it invites the heavens, the seas, the fields and the trees to sing and rejoice, and it ends with the reminder that he will judge the world.

Psalm 97 closes with two commands: "Rejoice in the Lord, you who are righteous, and praise his holy name."

Psalm 98 says "Shout for joy to the Lord, all the earth, burst into jubilant song with music".

Psalm 101 says "I will sing of your love and justice; to you, O Lord, I will sing praise".

Psalm 103 opens with the words "Praise the Lord, O my soul; all my inmost being praise his holy name", and it reminds us of how he forgives us, heals us, redeems us, crowns us with love and satisfies us with good things.

These and other psalms remind us to sing his praise, to thank him for his gifts, to be humble before him; and they remind us of how great he is as Creator and how much he has done for us. What matters in worship is that we should be looking to God. Our whole attention should be focused on him, and these psalms or other songs and hymns can help us to get into that frame of mind.

But there is nothing wrong with worship in different styles. The Quakers in their meetings use silence to focus on God. The Anglo-Catholics use ritual. The Charismatic worshippers may well sing and dance. One old lady said that there are many roads to God, but the Church of England is, as it were, the M1. We might agree with the first half of her statement; and we might even agree with the second half, when we take into account all the road works and speed restrictions on that motorway!

Worship can change and empower us, as we see in the following instances:

- The walls of Jericho fell down as the Israelites marched round, blew the trumpets and raised a great shout (Joshua 6.15-16).
- A few centuries later, when a strong army came against Jerusalem, King Jehoshaphat and the people prayed in their desperation. Then one of those present received a prophetic word "The battle is not yours but God's"; so

they praised and worshipped God, and the next day the battle was won without them having to strike a blow (2 Chronicles 20.12-23).

- Later still, after the return from exile, Nehemiah encouraged the people with the words "The joy of the Lord is your strength". We sometimes quote these words without noticing that they had just been praising and worshipping the Lord, listening to the Book of the Law and repenting as they were convicted by the reading (Nehemiah 8.1-10): this is the context within which the joy of the Lord can become our strength.

- In the New Testament, after the day of Pentecost the new believers spent time together in praise and teaching and sharing their possessions, all of which had a great effect on the growth of the early church.

In a book by Matt Redman* there are some striking examples of worship transforming situations and empowering people. Chase was two and a half years old when he was diagnosed with a rare brain tumour for which there was no known cure. He needed many months of treatment, but the family used to sing worship songs as they drove into hospital and waited in procedure rooms. They shared the song "10,000 Reasons" with the doctors and nurses, and it was often the last thing Chase heard at night before going to sleep. Then there was the couple who lost their young daughter in a horrible accident: they asked Matt Redman to sing the song "Blessed be Your Name" at the memorial service, and still managed to sing and cling on to God in the face of their tragic loss. Most moving of all were the men in prison in Indonesia who grew in faith as they waited for a probable death sentence: they were still singing the song "10,000 Reasons" at the very moment they faced the firing squad. Those are just a few of the stories in this remarkable book illustrating the powerful effect of worship on people's lives.

Can one worship even from the depths of a prison cell? Paul and Silas did. The Rumanian Pastor Richard Wurmbrand did, dancing for joy even though the guards thought he was going mad and brought him extra food. So did Brother Yun, singing Psalm 150 and finding that it filled him with joy and gradually conquered the coldness of the cell.** We may or may not face such extreme tests. But wherever we are, and however dire our situation, worship can be truly life-transforming.

For reading:
2 Chronicles 20.1-23

For discussion:
a) Do we praise God enough?
b) What do you find most helps you to worship God?
c) Should we prepare, and how can we prepare, for times when our faith will be tested?

---

*   "10,000 Reasons" by Matt Redman with Craig Borlase, published by David C Cook, 2016. See too Charlie's story which is referred to in the chapter "Confidence in the Face of Death".

** See Acts 16.25 and www.caseyhobbs.com/2011/10/25/dancing-in-chains-richard-wurmbrand-persecution-and-joy and www.inspirational christians.org/biography/brother-yun

15

Confidence in Luke

MATTHEW, MARK, LUKE AND JOHN - the names trip off the tongue in one breath, and the four Gospel writers do indeed complement each other. But Luke stands out among them for some remarkable and unique features.

Luke was a Gentile - probably the only non-Jew among the New Testament writers. He sets his work firmly in the context of the 1st century AD Roman Empire, for example by naming six Roman governors of Judea and three Roman Emperors (Augustus, Tiberius and Claudius - the other Gospel writers name none). Paul refers to him as "our dear friend Luke, the doctor" (Colossians 4.14), so he must have been a well educated man. The Gospel of Luke and the book Acts clearly come from the same author: both have introductions addressing a gentleman called Theophilus. Presumably Luke intended that these books would take the history of Christianity right through from the birth of Jesus to the early sixties when Paul's missionary journeys round the Mediterranean world were coming to a close. Luke had accompanied Paul on some of those journeys, as we see in three passages in Acts where "they" suddenly becomes "we" (chapters 16, 20-21 and 27-28).

He wrote in a polished style and in excellent Greek, and he is highly praised as a historian by modern scholars. "Luke's history is unsurpassed in respect of its trustworthiness".* "Luke is a historian of the first rank; not merely are his statements of fact trustworthy; he is possessed of the true historic sense; he fixes his mind on the idea and plan that rules in the evolution of history, and proportions the scale of his treatment to the importance of each incident...This author should be placed along with the very greatest of historians".** "Luke is a consummate historian, to be ranked in his own right with the great writers of the Greeks".*** Finally the eminent Roman historian A. N. Sherwin-White said of Acts: "Any attempt to reject its basic historicity, even in matters of detail, must now appear absurd".****

Several points from Luke's introduction to his Gospel (Luke 1.1-4) tie in with these judgments. He is aware of many other writers who have written about the life and ministry of Jesus (verse 1). He has consulted eye-witnesses (2). He has himself "carefully investigated everything from the beginning" (3). He wants to write an orderly account (3). He wants Theophilus to "know the certainty of the things you have been taught" (4).

There are striking parallels here with the highly respected Greek historian Thucydides, who wrote a history of the Peloponnesian War, the great war between Athens and Sparta, 431-404 BC. Like Luke, Thucydides was aware of the work of other writers (and he admitted they might be more colourful and entertaining than his own work, but not as useful); he too stressed the importance of eye-witnesses and the need for accuracy; he too had played a part in some of the events he describes; he too was writing so that posterity would know the truth of what actually happened (see Thucydides 1.22.1-4).

Luke takes great care over titles of officials, a minefield of complications where he might easily have made mistakes. There are the *proconsuls* of Cyprus, Achaia and Asia; the *magistrates* and their *officers* in the Roman colony of Philippi; the *politarchs* ("*city officials*" in the NIV) in Thessalonica; and *the first man of the island* ("*chief official*" in the NIV) in Malta (see Acts 13.7; 18.12; 19.38; 16.35; 17.6; 28.7).

Luke is also very precise about chronology, as we can see in Luke 2.2 and 3.1-2. The most useful parallel date given here is "the 15th year of the reign of Tiberius Caesar". Tiberius was Emperor from 14 to 37 AD, so we can date the start of the ministries of John the Baptist and Jesus to 28 AD. The passage about Gallio (Acts 18.12) is also hugely important. An inscription found at Delphi in the 1880s but not fully understood till 1907 confirms that Gallio became proconsul of Achaia in July 51 AD. This helped to date events in the life of Paul much more precisely, particularly his first visit to Corinth.

The mention of Quirinius (Luke 2.2) is thought to be a mistake. We know that he was governor of Syria in 6 AD and that there was a census then; but this is far too late for the birth of Jesus in the reign of King Herod, who murdered the babies in the Bethlehem area and then died in 4 BC. (So Jesus must have been born by 4 BC, and the 6th century monk who worked back to calculate the year of his birth got the BC/AD divide wrong by several years.) But people have not looked at the Greek text with sufficient care. The word "first" strongly suggests that there were two censuses and that Quirinius was in command in Syria twice, the first time being when he was conducting a war against a local tribe around 6 BC. At present historians cannot reach 100% certainty on these points, but I believe that Luke, with his fine record of accuracy elsewhere, deserves our trust here too.

For reading:
Luke 1.1-4; Acts 1.1-5

For discussion:
a) What would be lost if Luke had never written Acts?
b) Where does historical accuracy rank in importance among the qualities of a Gospel writer?
c) What impression of Luke as a person and a writer do we get when we look at the passages which only occur in his Gospel, for example details of the births of John the Baptist and Jesus (Luke chapters 1 and 2), the parables about the lost sheep, the lost coin and the lost son (Luke 15), and the Emmaus Road story (Luke 24.13-35)?

---

* W.Ramsay: Luke the Physician pp177-179; Hodder and Stoughton 1909.
** W.Ramsay: The Bearing of Recent Discovery on the Trustworthiness of the New Testament p 222, Hodder and Stoughton 1915.
*** E.M Blaiklock: The Acts of the Apostles p89, Tyndale Press 1959.
**** Roman Society and Roman Law in the New Testament p189, Clarendon Press 1963.

16

Confidence in Spite of War and Terrorism

WE'RE DOOMED...DON'T PANIC...NOWHERE'S SAFE...WHERE WILL it all end...Why doesn't God do something? These are some of the thoughts racing through people's minds as war rages or the latest act of terrorism appears on our TV screens. The shootings in Paris, the man forced to flee from war in Syria and then losing his wife and all his children when the boat capsized - sometimes it seems the forces of evil and selfishness are too strong, and nothing can be done to stop them.

We need a completely different perspective. We need to remind ourselves of at least four important truths: that God has not given up on the world, that evil will not always triumph, that there may well be suffering on the way through life, but that death is not the end.

1. God has not given up on the world. The most famous verse in the Bible says that "God so loved the world..." (John 3.16). He sent his Son into a dangerous world: King Herod was so worried about stories of a new-born king that he tried to destroy him by murdering all the young children in the Bethlehem area. Later Jesus said "You will hear of wars and rumours of wars, but see to it that you are not alarmed...

Nation will rise against nation...There will be famines and earthquakes in various places." (Matthew 24.6-7). So his disciples in any age should not be surprised on the many occasions when they see his words coming true. Jesus wept at the grave of Lazarus, recognising the pain and grief that the family was feeling (John 11.35). War and suffering do not take God by surprise. He feels our pain; he shares it; and he is still at work in a world of war, terrorism and crime, seeking to draw us back to himself.

2. Evil will not always triumph. It may seem that way at the moment; but the book of Revelation paints a very different picture of heavenly warfare, of the destruction of death, Hades and the forces of evil, and of the wonder of the new heaven and the new earth (Revelation 21-22). Revelation helps to correct our distorted vision; it shows us what is really going on; it is like turning over a mass of tangled threads and finding a beautiful tapestry on the other side.

3. There may well be suffering on the way through life. No one, whether Christian or not, is immune. Christianity is the most persecuted religion on the planet at present. In many places Christians are denied justice, denied work opportunities, denied the right to meet together or to talk openly about their faith, their churches are burned down, their children are kidnapped and they themselves are violently attacked. None of this can be endured or make any sense at all *unless* there is a deeper reality behind all the suffering, a God who cares, who sustains and who will ultimately put all things right. But if we do believe in that reality, the most important thing in the world is not to hold on to life at all costs, but to walk with God, to stay close to him, to trust him whatever happens. Even if we are faced with the prospect of what some people call the ultimate sacrifice, we shouldn't give up in fear or

despair: Jesus said "Do not be afraid of those who kill the body and after that can do no more. But I will show you whom you should fear: Fear him who, after the killing of the body, has power to throw you into hell" (Luke 12.4-5).

4. Death is not the end. There is grief at a funeral, and anger too when it is a younger person who has been killed through war, terrorism, an accident or an incurable illness. But Jesus said "I am the resurrection and the life" and "In my Father's house are many rooms" (John 11.25, 14.2). He conquered death on the first Easter Sunday, and he offers eternal life to those who believe in him.

Peter saw Jesus walking on water. He could walk on water too, as long as he kept looking at Jesus. But when he looked down at the waves he started sinking (Matthew 14.25-31). Like the writer of Psalm 121, we need to get a totally new perspective: "I lift up my eyes to the hills - where does my help come from? My help comes from the Lord, the Maker of heaven and earth".

For reading:
Matthew 24.1-14; Acts 7.54-60; 2 Timothy 4.6-8

For discussion:
a) Are the forces of evil winning - or have they already won?
b) How easy do we find it to adopt a Christian view of death?
c) Looking at 2 Timothy 4.6-8, what motivated Paul and inspired him to live the way he lived?

17

Confidence in Eschatology – another conversation from 221 B Baker Street

"**E**SCHATOLOGY, MY DEAR WATSON!"

"I beg your pardon, Holmes? Did you sneeze?"

"No, Watson. I was merely breaking in on your thought processes and telling you that eschatology was the answer."

"But hold on, isn't that the study of the obscene bits in Greek Comedy? I'm sure I remember reading some Aristophanes at school before I turned to studying Medicine. And what on earth that has to do with my thought processes I simply can't imagine."

"No, Watson, that is scatology – a very different field of study, and not one I would want to link to your train of thought."

"So what are you talking about then, and anyway, how can you read what's going on in my mind?"

"Eschatology is the doctrine of the last things, the consummation of human history, what happens at the end of the world. And, Watson, your expressions and actions in the last five minutes are like an open book. Let me explain. You started by leafing through your family photograph album. You smiled. Then you turned a page and a look of sadness came over you. You must have been thinking of your poor unfortunate brother, especially as you then patted his watch which now sits in your waistcoat pocket. Then you reached for the dictionary and looked up two entries in the first third of the alphabet. You raised your eyebrows, turned back to the photo album and looked thoughtful. Is it too hard to deduce you were looking at the entries for death and heaven, and pondering the mystery of what happens after death?"

"Holmes, you are amazing! I shall have to put up a screen and hide my facial expressions from you in future. But I had no idea that you were an expert on eschatology. Tell me more."

"Well, Watson, we are talking here about the Four Last Things – Death, Judgment, Heaven and Hell. We are talking about the final events of history and the ultimate destiny of mankind. The Second Coming of Christ is the central event in Christian eschatological thinking. He entered this world once, as a tiny baby, but he will come again in power and glory. And I should warn you, Watson, that a great deal of nonsense is bandied about on these topics."

"You mean people like that man down the street carrying a sandwich board saying the end is near?"

"Precisely. He *may* just be right, by co-incidence; but it's quite clear from Jesus's words in Matthew 24.36 that no-one except God the Father knows in advance the precise time of the Second Coming and the end of the world. We should also note the warnings earlier in that chapter about false Christs and false prophets deceiving people.

"However, we *are* living in what the Bible calls the last times, even though it doesn't make clear how long those last times will be. "In these last days he [God] has spoken to us by his Son." "He [Jesus] was chosen before the creation of the world, but was revealed in these last times for your sake." "Dear children, this is the last hour." You can find those passages in Hebrews 1.2, 1 Peter 1.20 and 1 John 2.18. The life of Jesus inaugurated the last times. Some writers talk of Realised or Inaugurated Eschatology (which began with Jesus' First Coming), as opposed to Future Eschatology (which concerns his Second Coming). But I think that sounds unnecessarily complicated!"

"I totally agree, Holmes. Let's keep it as simple as possible. Could we examine the Four Last Things?"

"We shall all face death one day, Watson, unless of course the Second Coming occurs first. And we have just one life. Reincarnation, which you probably read about in the Roman poet Virgil at school, may sound a lovely idea, but it is not Biblical: read Hebrews 9.27, which talks about humans dying once and after that facing judgment.

"So what about judgment? You probably remember the parable of the sheep and the goats in Matthew 25. But it's not really a parable at all, just a straightforward piece of teaching. All the nations will be gathered before the throne of the Son of man, and he will separate them *as a shepherd separates the sheep from the goats.* It's a simile, not a parable, and the rest of the passage talks in plain language about judgment and separation. And does this happen instantly, immediately after death? Or is it like waking from sleep, so that judgment will only *seem* instant? We don't know, and we don't need to know.

"And then heaven. Heaven is where God is. It's being with him for ever. Jesus on the cross said to the dying but penitent thief "Today you will be with me in paradise", and paradise is a word which is rich with meaning."

"Yes, Holmes, I discovered this the other day. It's a word of Persian origin, meaning a garden. And it has just occurred to me, that takes us right back to Genesis 3 and the Garden of Eden. Someone at my Club was saying that being admitted to paradise is a reversal of the exclusion of Adam and Eve from the garden at the start of the Bible."

"Very good, Watson. And human salvation is intimately tied up with the liberation of creation. At present we see a world that is spoiled and subject to *its bondage to decay*, as Paul called it in Romans 8.21. But it will be set free: there will be a new heaven and a new earth. No more London fogs, Watson – think of that!

"But I fear we must also think about hell. Jesus talked about unquenchable fire (Mark 9.43 and 48 if you want to look it up), and about a place of darkness, regret and weeping (in Matthew 8.12). The book Revelation talks of the lake of fire which is the second death, for those whose names are not written in the book of life (see Revelation 20.14). There are also those sobering words about entering through the narrow gate – not the wide gate and the broad road that leads to destruction: that's Matthew 7.13. Some people argue about whether hell means eternal punishment or eternal destruction; but I think it is more important to focus on making the right choice than on wondering about the consequences of the wrong choice. And by the way, don't let anyone talk you into believing that universalism is true – the belief that everyone is saved in the end. Jesus says in that passage in Matthew 7 (and you can almost hear the sorrow in his voice) that only a few find the narrow road."

"Thank you, Holmes. That all seems very clear. Is there anything else I should know?"

"Yes and no Watson. You know how I hate speculation without evidence. Some people talk a lot about the millennium mentioned in Revelation 20. But this is the only passage in the whole Bible that talks about that period of 1000 years, which anyway sounds more like a symbolic than a literal number. Amillennialism, premillennialism, postmillennialism – there's no consensus among the experts, and it all sounds to me like theorising with insufficient data.

"Others get excited about the Rapture, though they don't all agree what that means. They link together 1 Thessalonians 4.17

with Matthew 24.40-41. But there are two completely different words for *caught up* or *taken* in those two passages. Paul in 1 Thessalonians 4 is talking about something good: believers who are still alive at the Second Coming will be *caught up* to meet the Lord in the air, along with those who have died and then been raised from the dead. Matthew 24 on the other hand is all about two future events, the destruction of Jerusalem by the Romans and the end of the world: the first of those events will be a time of tribulation and of people being *taken away* for captivity or punishment, and he draws a parallel with the time of Noah and the people who got *caught* by the flood. Really, Watson, there is so much speculation and nonsense around. Why can't they look at the evidence? Why can't they analyse the language more carefully? Sometimes I despair of the so-called experts!"

For reading:
1 Corinthians 15.35-58

For discussion:
a) What are the things that have most surprised you in the discussion above?
b) How important is it to have a clear understanding of the Four Last Things?
c) Why do so few choose the narrow gate described in Matthew 7.13-14?

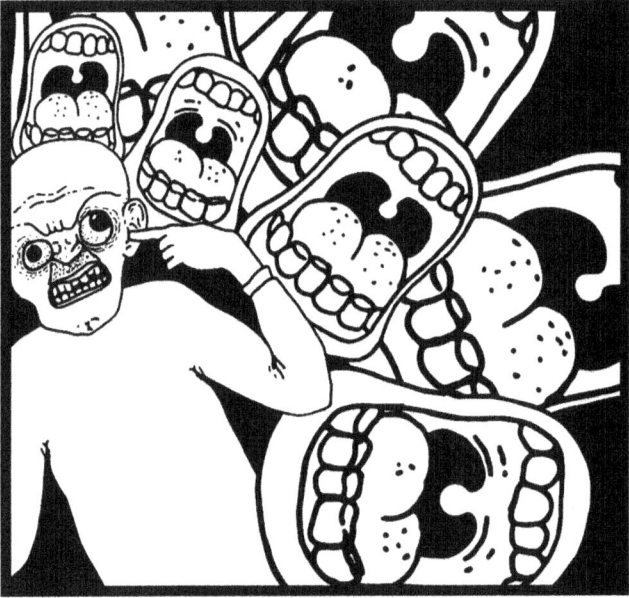

AT THE EVENING SERVICE TONIGHT
THE SERMON TOPIC WILL BE "WHAT IS HELL?"
COME EARLY AND LISTEN TO OUR CHOIR PRACTICE.

18

Confidence in Reading the Bible

Is reading the Bible a complete waste of time? When we open it, are we tuning in to the Creator of the universe, the one who loves us and has a plan for our lives? Or are we wasting time on an old and irrelevant book of lies, myths and legends? Here are ten suggestions: we should read the Bible...

1. **To find the way to God** - All religions are humans searching for God by their own efforts. In the Bible God is searching for us and showing us why we are out of touch with him and how to find him again. We need God's words, not human wisdom: Paul wrote to Timothy "From infancy you have known the holy Scriptures, which are able to make you wise for salvation through faith in Christ Jesus."

2. **To find the answer to death** - Jesus said "I am the resurrection and the life. He who believes in me will live, even though he dies." So physical death is not the end: it is the gateway to eternal joy for those who trust in Jesus. And if we are afraid of dying, we can hold on to King David's words "Even though I walk through the valley of the shadow of death, I will fear no evil, for you are with me."

3. **To find firm foundations in life** - Jesus told a story about two
people who built houses: one house had good foundations,
while the other was built on sand and soon collapsed.
"Everyone who hears these words of mine and puts them into
practice is like a wise man who built his house on the rock."
There is the point of the story: we are unwise if we pay no
attention to Jesus' words, for then we have no foundations.

4. **To find genuine happiness** - The writer of Ecclesiastes
(King Solomon?) wrote "Utterly meaningless! Everything
is meaningless. What does man gain from all his labour
at which he toils under the sun?" He found that all life's
pleasures, like study or laughter or wine or great building
projects, were ultimately dissatisfying, unless we remember
our Creator. Only in God can we find true satisfaction; and
how can we find God except through his word, the Bible?

5. **To find the explanation for human wickedness** - Why is
there so much war, greed, crime and violence in the world?
Some people claim that mankind is gradually getting better;
but the Bible gives a more realistic diagnosis. "Men loved
darkness instead of light because their deeds were evil."
Whether we read Old Testament history, or the Prophets, or
the Gospels, we find the same answer: it is all due to human
selfishness.

6. **To find answers to difficult questions** - What is God like?
How can God be three persons and yet one? What exactly is
the Gospel message? What about the Devil? What is heaven
like? What happens to those who have never heard of Jesus?
We can make guesses using our own human wisdom; but
it is much better to go to the source book and find the true
answers. Clearly the Psalmist studied God's word: he wrote
"I have more insight than all my teachers, for I meditate on
your statutes".

7. **To help others find faith** - Peter wrote "Always be prepared to give an answer to everyone who asks you to give the reason for the hope you have"; and the book of Proverbs says "The mind of the righteous ponders how to answer". In the Bible we discover what we need to say; and as it is inspired by God, it is more powerful than our own words in explaining sin, the cross and repentance.

8. **To find guidance in life** - We can find general principles (like "Good sense makes a man slow to anger" or "Love your enemies and pray for those who persecute you"). But at times we need directions now (Which subjects should I study? What career should I follow? Should I take on that leadership role?). It is surprising how, when we ask God for guidance, a verse can sometimes leap off the page and be his answer.

9. **To find comfort in times of pain, sorrow or illness** - Instead of asking why did it happen to me, read the Psalms (like Psalm 23), or see how people in the Bible faced suffering. King Hezekiah came to see beyond his immediate illness: "Surely it was for my benefit that I suffered such anguish. In your love you kept me from the pit of destruction". And Paul three times pleaded with God to take away his thorn in the flesh (we don't know exactly what it was) but God replied "My grace is sufficient for you, for my power is made perfect in weakness".

10. **To find God's agenda for local churches** - In Acts chapter 13 the church in Antioch felt called to send out Paul and Barnabas on a special missionary journey. Every group of believers is unique and faces different situations. What is God calling *us* to do here in our city/town/village? Do we need to pray together more, or start a lunch club for the elderly, or welcome refugees, or run meetings for businessmen? As we pray and study the Bible, God will speak about our particular situation.

If these are strong reasons for studying the Bible, it follows that reading the Bible is one of the most important activities we can do each day. So if you already read it regularly, keep going with confidence. If you have got stuck or haven't really started yet, it's never too late to begin.

For reading:

These are the verses quoted in the ten paragraphs above: 2 Timothy 3.15; John 11.25 and Psalm 23.4; Matthew 7.24-27; Ecclesiastes 1.2-3; John 3.19; Psalm 119.99; 1 Peter 3.15 and Proverbs 15.28 (RSV); Proverbs 19.11 (RSV) and Matthew 5.44; Isaiah 38.17 and 2 Corinthians 12.7-9; Acts 13.1-3. See too Colossians 3.16; 2 Timothy 3.10-17.

For discussion:

a) Which do you think are the most important reasons for reading the Bible?

b) How important is regularity? Is it like brushing teeth or practising the piano?

c) What helpful hints would you give to someone who wants to make a start on the Bible?

19

Confidence in the Love of God

WHAT IS GOD LIKE? A stern policeman, a kindly uncle, a weak and tired old man with a long beard, or a monster and a megalomaniac? There are all sorts of interesting or weird ideas around in popular thinking and in modern atheist writers. Are all these ideas equally valid, or is there some more reliable source of information?

Someone once said, if you want to know what God is like, look at Jesus. It's good advice: Jesus himself said "Anyone who has seen me has seen the Father", while Paul wrote "The Son is the image of the invisible God", and the writer of the letter called Hebrews said "The Son is the radiance of God's glory and the exact representation of his being" (John 14.9, Colossians 1.15, Hebrews 1.3).

When we read the Gospels, we find someone who was kind, gentle and loving. He was compassionate (like when he said to the dying thief on the cross "Today you will be with me in paradise"), stern sometimes (like when he drove the traders out of the Temple) and challenging and demanding sometimes (like when he challenged a rich young ruler to go and sell all his possessions and follow him). We find someone who voluntarily faced an agonising death in order to rescue us: "The Son of Man did not come to be served, but to serve, and to give his life as a ransom for many" and "God so loved the world that he gave his one and only Son, that whoever believes in him shall not perish but have eternal life" (Mark 10.45, John 3.16).

There are four "God is" statements in the New Testament - God is light, God is love, God is spirit, and God is a consuming fire.* We must not forget that he is a God of holiness, purity, judgment and justice. But the statement "God is love" reminds us that he is utterly loving: love is part of his essential nature. The American writer Philip Yancey said "We need to let it soak in that there is nothing we can do to make God love us more...and nothing we can do to make God love us less".**

So how does it work out in practice? What difference does it make believing God loves us? It's easy to believe God loves us when things are going well and he seems to be smiling on us. There is a deep underlying joy, confidence and certainty. Paul wrote "Rejoice in the Lord always. I will say it again: rejoice!" (Philippians 4.4), and it is sometimes easy to put that command into practice. But what about those times of doubts and uncertainty, or illness, or extreme danger?

If we are full of doubts or uncertain about the future, that doesn't alter his love for us. "If we are faithless, he will remain faithful, for he cannot disown himself" (2 Timothy 2.13). God has his perfect plans, even if at first we don't understand them. One example is in Acts chapter 8, where Philip was engaged in fruitful work spreading the message in Samaria and must have wondered why on earth God was suddenly sending him down a desert road to the south. However he was in exactly the right place at the right time to meet an important Ethiopian official on his way home from a festival in Jerusalem. This man had bought a scroll of the prophet Isaiah and was puzzled as he read chapter 53; but Philip was able to explain that the passage referred to Jesus, and he helped him to find true faith and joy. Sometimes it is the amazing coincidences and God's careful planning that convince me that he really loves us.

If we are ill, or crushed by some heavy disappointment, those are often the times when God can get our attention - even when we are shouting Why, why, why? Paul suffered what he called a thorn in the flesh, some weakness or long-term illness, though he doesn't specify exactly what it was. At first he kept praying for God to take it away, but eventually he came to see it as part of God's perfect plan for him: see 2 Corinthians 12.7-10.

And if we are in extreme danger, maybe facing death - or even more agonisingly seeing our children martyred for their faith, as is happening right now elsewhere in the world - we can remember that death is not the end: remember Revelation 2.10 "Be faithful, even to the point of death, and I will give you life as your victor's crown". At the Last Supper Jesus told his disciples "As the Father has loved me, so have I loved you", and he has gone ahead to prepare a place in heaven for his followers (John 15.9 and John 14.2-3). As Paul assures us in Romans 8.38-39, nothing, not even death, can separate us from the love of God.

For reading:

Psalm 23.1; Deuteronomy 7.6-11; John 10.10-15; 1 John 4.18-19

For discussion:

a) What do these passages tell us about God's love?

b) Do we find it hard to believe that God loves us?

c) Why/Why not?

---

* They can be found in 1 John 1.5, 1 John 4.8, John's Gospel 4.24 and Hebrews 12.29 (which is a quote from Deuteronomy 4.24).

** See the website philipyancey.com/q-and-a-topics/grace

20

Confidence in Eternal Life

A MAN ONCE RUSHED UP TO his vicar in a state of great agitation. "Vicar, vicar, I'm terribly worried. Are there golf courses in heaven?" The vicar replied that he would pray about it. Two days later he came back with an answer. "I've got good news and bad news. The good news is that there are golf courses in heaven. The bad news is that you are booked for your first round this Saturday at 9am!"

Is that what eternal life is about – an extension of all the pleasures we have enjoyed in this life? I suspect that man was asking the wrong question. So what is heaven all about? Some people have a mental picture of harps and haloes and endless singing, and they think that sounds boring.

But the Bible hints at something far better, even though it doesn't give full details. Jesus said "In my Father's house are many rooms; if it were not so, I would have told you. I am going there to prepare a place for you" (John 14.2). And Paul wrote "No eye has seen, no ear has heard, no mind has conceived what God has prepared for those who love him" (1 Corinthians 2.9). The word *prepare* occurs in both those passages. Everything has been made ready; and since God has already created an amazing universe, it is entirely fitting to believe that even better things await his servants after they have passed from this world.

In the last book of the Bible John writes of the new heaven and new earth, a place with no more tears, death or pain (Revelation 21.1-4). It is a place where the river of the water of life flows, with the tree of life bearing different crops of fruit each month, "and the leaves of the tree are for the healing of the nations" (Revelation 22.1-2). In a world of conflict, violence and famine where many people lack clean drinking water, that description sounds wonderful beyond words.

Furthermore eternal life is not just reserved for some distant point in the future. It starts now. Jesus said to his disciples "I tell you the truth, whoever hears my word and believes him who sent me has eternal life and will not be condemned; he has crossed over from death to life" (John 5.24). The verbs here are important. The believer "has eternal life", and that means now. He or she "will not be condemned" in the future, on the Day of Judgment, but "has crossed over from death to life": the transition has already taken place. The same point is made in John 3.36: "Whoever believes in the Son has eternal life, but whoever rejects the Son will not see life, for God's wrath remains on him". The simple certainty of the language is striking, and the choice is very clear. And how do we move from death to life? Again we find the answer in John's Gospel: "God so loved the world that he gave his one and only Son, that whoever believes in him shall not perish but have eternal life" (John 3.16). We need to believe in Jesus – not just believe that he existed, but believe and entrust ourselves to him, the one who was given to the world to face an agonising death on the cross so that he could win forgiveness for us. The alternative to believing is perishing – missing out on eternal life.

One of the two thieves who were crucified with Jesus recognised that there was something special about him. He said, and it sounds rather wistful, "Jesus, remember me when you come into your kingdom"; and immediately he got the answer "I tell you the truth, today you will be with me in paradise" (Luke 23.42-43). There was no difference between what the thief said and what anyone can pray now: a simple sentence opened the gateway to eternal life.

And John implies that this new life is wonderful. "The thief comes only to steal and kill and destroy; I have come that they may have life, and have it to the full" (John 10.10). Abundant life, life in all its fullness – does this mean now or hereafter? The answer is both.

So what happens at death? Paul talks about the resurrection of the body in 1 Corinthians 15. Since Jesus was raised from the dead, we too will be raised. How will this happen? It will be like a seed falling into the ground, dying and growing up into a new body. It will be a spiritual body (verse 44), changed in the twinkling of an eye (51-52), immortal and imperishable (53-54), conquering death and turning it into victory (54-57).

Paul doesn't give us a complete picture: he cannot go into more detail than he has done here, and he makes no mention of golf courses, or whatever was the first century equivalent of golf! But perhaps we can put it like this: there will either be golf courses in heaven or something much, much better.

For reading:
John 10.22-29

For discussion:
   a)   What do you understand by the words "eternal life"?
   b)   How would you explain to someone how to find eternal life?
   c)   Why do some people find it so hard to accept the words of Jesus?

21

Confidence in the Goodness of God

I T'S A REAL PROBLEM: ANYONE who says God is good and loving has to attempt to make sense of all the evil and suffering in the world. Ebola, terrorism, child abuse, crime, sex trafficking, cyclones, earthquakes, homelessness...the list is endless. In the face of all that and much more, can we really believe in the goodness and love of God?

This could be just an academic question - an interesting philosophical discussion, or a barrier for those exploring the Christian faith. For the atheists it is perhaps the strongest argument they have that there is no God, or at least not the God portrayed in the Bible. If God really is loving and all-powerful, surely he can remove evil with just a word of command; so evil and suffering prove that he is either unloving or too weak, or both.

You can find an interview with Stephen Fry on Youtube: he was asked what he would say if he came face to face with God. His answer has been watched and commented on by millions. "Bone cancer in children? What's that about? How dare you? How dare you create a world in which there is such misery that is not our fault? It's not right. It's utterly, utterly evil. Why should I respect a capricious, mean-minded, stupid God who creates a world which is so full of injustice and pain..." How should we respond? Have we *any* counter-arguments, or has the time come to admit that the atheists have won the argument?

We have to admit right at the outset that there is no easy answer. Somebody once said "The book on suffering doesn't exist". In other words we will never be able to give a complete answer to the problem of evil. But even if we can't say *everything*, we can at least say *something*. We need to sharpen our thinking.

Firstly, Jesus shared our suffering. Illegitimate birth, exile, hunger, thirst, tiredness, rejection, injustice, mockery and an agonising death - he faced it all. He doesn't wash his hands of us when things go wrong. He has first-hand experience of suffering, and he promised to be with his followers every step of the way: "Surely I am with you always..." (Matthew 28.20).

Secondly, suffering can often draw people nearer to God: it is his megaphone, as C.S.Lewis put it, to waken a world which is deafened by pleasure. It may prompt us to spend more time seeking God in prayer, something we didn't make time for when all was going well. When we pray for help for ourselves or for someone else, whether there is a quick and positive answer or not, prayer changes us for the better.

Thirdly, the suffering of others can make us more kind, thoughtful and caring; whereas undiluted pleasure and happiness will tend to make us selfish. Later in his interview Stephen Fry referred to insects that cause children to go blind: for him that is yet more convincing proof that God is evil. But this should be not a debating point: it should be a call for rich nations and wealthy individuals to provide more medical help. What are human greed and selfishness doing about malaria, which is still one of the world's biggest killers? In the face of tsunamis, earthquakes, floods and droughts, why aren't rich nations more effective in distributing food, medicine and safe housing fairly? Where does the fault lie?

Next, even if our prayers seem to be unanswered, death is not the end. The world sees nothing beyond this life, and it looks on pain, illness and death as things to be avoided as much as possible. But for the Christian death should not be the elephant in the room, the ultimate tragedy we try not to mention; rather it is the gateway to a much better life. John 3.16 is probably the most famous verse in the Bible: it makes clear that all a person has to do is to believe and so accept God's gift of eternal life.

What about children, then? Aren't they too young to understand and accept this gift? In the Gospels Jesus welcomed children; therefore I believe that those who die as babies or small children (or even unborn foetuses) go straight to heaven.

Illness and death entered the world because of man's sin. Genesis 1 describes God's perfect creation. Then in Genesis 3 comes the Fall - mankind's rebellion against God. That disobedience not only caused a rift between us and God but also in a strange way affected the whole of creation, as Paul explains in Romans 8.21-22. This is a mystery. Could God have created a better world, a world without freewill, or a free world with no evil? Or would that have made us just robots? We don't know, and the existence of evil is one of the many problems we cannot understand fully: if we could, we would be greater than God.

We have been exploring the problem of suffering in general, as an academic question. But for some people it is a much more personal question - why me? Why was I always picked on at school? Why have I been made redundant? Why did my little brother have to die so young? Why does my mother suffer from dementia? Why is it my kids who are going off the rails? Others are probably more qualified than I am to speak on these issues; but such questions deserve an answer, and we shall examine the personal impact of suffering in the next chapter.

For reading:
Genesis 3.17-19; Job chapters 1, 2 and 3; Romans 8.18-25

For discussion:
a) How much of the world's suffering and evil is man's fault rather than God's?
b) "Human suffering proves that God is not all-powerful, or not all-loving." True?
c) Do we pay attention to our eternal destiny and to the time when all suffering will be past?

22

Confidence When Life Gets Tough

IT'S ALL VERY WELL TO talk in a detached way about God's goodness whatever happens in life; but what about those times when tragedy strikes us personally?

Horatio Spafford was an American lawyer with extensive property in Chicago, till he was ruined financially by the great fire in 1871. He suffered further losses in the economic downturn of 1873, when he had already decided to travel to Europe. Delayed by sorting out his business interests, he sent his wife Anna and their four daughters on ahead in the SS Ville du Havre. But the vessel suffered a mid-Atlantic collision and sank quickly, after which his wife sent a telegram with the sad message "Saved alone...". In the face of such heart-rending news, Horatio sailed for Europe to comfort his grieving wife; and as he was passing near the spot where his daughters had drowned, he felt moved to pen a wonderful hymn of faith:

> When peace like a river attendeth my way,
> when sorrows like sea-billows roll;
> whatever my lot You have taught me to say,
> It is well, it is well with my soul...

How would we have faced such a tragedy? For some people suffering leads to bitterness; for others it awakens even deeper trust in the God who loves us, suffers with us and ultimately knows what is best for us.

One of Justin Welby's last engagements as Bishop of Durham a few years ago was to speak at a Carol Service at All Saints Preston on Tees. He told us about the anguish of losing his seven-month-old daughter after a car accident in France; of how he walked the streets praying for her and then looked up and saw a sign "Let the little children come to me", and he just knew that Johanna was going to die - yet he did not give up on God, and is quoted as saying "It was a very dark time for my wife Caroline and myself, but in a strange way it actually brought us closer to God."

Other stories can easily be found locally - less spectacular, maybe, but painful for those who had to live through these circumstances. Here are five, with names changed to protect identities.

Mary writes: "Twice in my Christian life I've suffered from a reactive depression. Once when it first happened I hadn't slept for 24 hours, so was exhausted, but I had a picture of a baby being held in huge, gentle hands. I realised that God was holding me and wanted me to know I was safe and loved. But apart from that instance, both periods of depression left me feeling very far from God. I knew he existed, I never lost my faith, but he felt far away. Part of this was because I didn't feel I could trust him or trust what I thought he was saying. It took some months, the second time, before I could open my hands in a physical gesture to receive from him again. Thankfully I have not got a depressive personality, but I can empathise more with those going thro' depression because of my experience. Depression is not just a mental issue. It is exhausting physically too."

John was 22 when two things happened in quick succession to rock his faith. He had been convinced that he was being called to be ordained, but the selection board unexpectedly turned him down; and then just after his university final exams he got a letter with results that were much worse than he had hoped for. It took time to get things in perspective - along with a really encouraging letter from a wise friend who wrote "Did you know that a translation of Zephaniah 3.17 says *He is silently planning in love for you?*"

Daniel is a Christian from Pakistan who at the time of writing is seeking asylum in this country. He has been turned down once and is appealing, as there is the threat of death hanging over him because of his faith if he has to return home. Meanwhile he is not allowed to work here, whether on a paid or a voluntary basis. But he is getting really well involved in his local church, investing time in studying for future jobs and seizing opportunities to be a Christian witness to people he meets.

Emily had to have treatment for cancer (still ongoing at the time of writing) but has faced it all very positively and found it has given her new opportunities to talk with people about the deepest issues of life and death. Some time after her diagnosis she was able to comment "I joined an exclusive club for which I didn't apply for membership".

Thomas writes: "When I got ill and it became apparent that it was not going away it hit my faith. Especially when the diagnosis came through that it was probably for life and I was unlikely to recover. I seriously doubted my faith and questioned what I had done or hadn't done that had upset the Lord and caused Him to give me my illness. However after a while my faith grew, especially as the curate at our church offered prayer for healing. Through that I slowly recovered but also my faith grew; Bible study become possible and I felt much closer to the Lord. I decided that my salary (which had been greatly reduced since I was on sick pay) should be properly tithed. My faith grew further as we have never since had to worry about our finances. Recently my faith has again been hit with the severe illness of a close loved one. But as it says in James 5:13-16 we should pray and that is what I do."

I hope these stories encourage us to press on, keep praying and not give up on God.

For reading:

2 Corinthians 1.8-11; 2 Corinthians 12.7-10; Galatians 6.2; Revelation 2.8-11

For discussion:

a) How can we cope better with "the slings and arrows of outrageous fortune" - illness, accident, bereavement, unemployment, loneliness, rejection, ostracism, slander, false accusation, persecution...?

b) What did Paul mean by "Carry one another's burdens"?

c) To what extent do we, or should we, live life on earth in the light of heaven?

23

Confidence in Ourselves

HAT? YOU CAN'T BE SERIOUS! Doesn't the Bible tell us in dozens of passages to be humble, to recognise our sinfulness and shortcomings, and not to boast about who we are and what we have achieved in life? Here is a list of reasons why we shouldn't have confidence in ourselves.

We can't rely on our own strength: Paul felt utterly crushed and near death at one stage in his travels. "But this happened that we might not rely on ourselves but on God" was the lesson he drew from this experience (2 Corinthians 1.8-11). It is the same in the Old Testament: "This is what the Lord says: Let not the wise man boast of his wisdom or the strong man boast of his strength or the rich man boast of his riches, but let him who boasts boast about this: that he understands and knows me…" (Jeremiah 9.23-24). Knowing the Lord and acting in his strength is the path to success.

We can't rely on our own health: King Herod in all his royal finery was enjoying the adulation of the crowd when his health suddenly gave way, for he did not give the glory to God (Acts 12.21-23). Even the great missionary Paul suffered from what he called a thorn in the flesh – it may have been eye trouble – which kept him humble, acknowledging his weakness and relying on God's strength (2 Corinthians 12.7-10). And his protégé Timothy had some sort of stomach trouble – maybe it was irritable bowel syndrome (1 Timothy 5.23). We never know what lies just round the corner.

We can't rely on our own life and plans for tomorrow: "Do not boast about tomorrow, for you do not know what a day may bring forth" (Proverbs 27.1). The letter of James is similarly scathing about those who make great plans for business and money-making and forget the brevity and uncertainty of life (James 4.13-16).

We can't rely on our own wealth: Jesus told a story about a rich man who thought that his abundant crops were the most important thing in his life, and who failed to pay any attention to God until it was too late (Luke 12.15-21). Paul gives similar instructions to Timothy: "Command those who are rich in this present world not to be arrogant nor to put their hope in wealth, which is so uncertain…" (1 Timothy 6.17).

We can't rely on our own achievements: The writer of Proverbs offers advice to those who are always talking about themselves: "Let another praise you, and not your own mouth, someone else, and not your own lips" (Proverbs 27.2). Jesus too forbids boasting, even about great things done in his service: when the 72 whom he had sent out to preach and heal return elated by their success, even to the extent of casting out demons, he warns them "Do not rejoice that the spirits submit to you, but rejoice that your names are written in heaven" (Luke 10.18-20).

We can't rely on our own righteousness: Everyone has sinned, says Paul. Everyone falls short of God's glory. We need his righteousness – we have none of our own – and we obtain it only by faith in Jesus (Romans 3.21-24). Peter says the same: "For Christ died for sins once for all, the righteous for the unrighteous, to bring you to God" (1 Peter 3.18).

We can't rely on our own innate goodness: Paul talks about a major internal struggle. He wants to do good, but for reasons he doesn't understand he finds himself always choosing to do the opposite (Romans 7.14-25). How surprising to read these words from one who endured and achieved so much in God's service. But he knew the reality and faced up to his inner weaknesses. Which of us can claim to do better, to live up to our own standards, let alone God's perfect standards?

There the case for the prosecution rests. We are not good enough. There are times when we could echo the words of the Psalm-writer: "I am a worm and not a man" (Psalm 22.6). Another Old Testament writer sounds even more gloomy: "How then can a man be righteous before God? If even the moon is not bright and the stars are not pure in his eyes, how much less man, who is but a maggot – a son of man, who is only a worm!" (Job 25.4-6). And yet, despite all these negatives, the Bible has some very positive things to say about our status before God and our role in his plans.

Firstly, we have been adopted as his children (Ephesians 1.5). What a privilege! The prologue in John's Gospel makes the same point: "To all who received him [Jesus], to those who believed in his name, he gave the right to become children of God" (John 1.12).

Secondly, Jesus spoke some amazingly encouraging words at the Last Supper: "I no longer call you servants, because a servant does not know his master's business. Instead, I have called you friends, for everything that I learned from my Father I have made known to you" (John 15.15). I am confident that these words apply not just to the original twelve disciples but to us too.

Thirdly, Jesus not only said he was the light of the world: he also said "You are the light of the world" (John 8.12; Matthew 5.14). He has entrusted his followers with a weighty responsibility!

Fourthly, he commissions his followers and sends them out. In Luke 10 we read of 72 being sent out to heal and to proclaim God's kingdom; and at the end of his time on earth he commissioned the eleven disciples to go out into all the world and to teach the new disciples to observe all the commands he had taught them (Matthew 28.16-20). Again, it is a weighty responsibility.

Following on from that point, we are Jesus' representatives. He says "He who listens to you listens to me; he who rejects you rejects me; but he who rejects me rejects him who sent me" (Luke 10.16).

Next, he gives his followers boldness. We read of this throughout the book Acts, but especially on the Day of Pentecost when Peter – the coward who had three times denied knowing Jesus only a few weeks before – spoke confidently to the crowds in Jerusalem to explain what had just happened (Acts 2.1-41).

Finally, we are all important, because we are all members of a body. The group of believers is like the human body: each person has a different gift and a function that helps and complements the rest of the body (Romans 12.4-8). Therefore no one should sit back and just be a passenger. No one should think they are too unimportant and unworthy to be included in the body of the church.

Summing up, we need to get the balance right between humility and confidence. There are pitfalls to avoid, but we have been granted a high status and important responsibility in God's service.

For reading:
Romans 12.1-8

For discussion:
a) Which do you see as the greater danger, excessive humility or over-confidence?
b) What exactly is Romans 12.3 saying about how we should view ourselves?
c) What gifts do you have, and what role is God calling you to play?

24

Confidence in the Value
of the Old Testament

WHAT IS THE OLD TESTAMENT? The first book, Genesis, starts with the accounts of Creation, the Fall, the spread of mankind, the Flood and the Tower of Babel. However most of the Old Testament focuses on the story of Israel. Starting with the call of Abraham in Genesis 12, it moves through the period of the Patriarchs (Abraham, Isaac and Jacob), exile in Egypt, the exodus from Egypt, wanderings in the desert, the arrival in the Promised Land, the period when judges like Samuel ruled Israel, the kings, the split between the Northern and Southern Kingdoms (Israel and Judah), the exile in Babylon, and finally the return from exile and the rebuilding of the Temple and the walls of Jerusalem. The Old Testament was the Bible for the Jews. Jesus referred to it when he said "Everything must be fulfilled that is written about me in the Law of Moses, the Prophets and the Psalms" (Luke 24.44). It is helpful to think in terms of a three-fold division between history (all the books from Genesis to Esther), wisdom (five books including Psalms and Proverbs) and prophecy (the four major and twelve minor prophets).

Why should we read the Old Testament today? If Jesus shows us what God is really like, if "the Son is the radiance of God's glory and the exact representation of his being" (Hebrews

1.3), surely there is no need to delve into the obscurities of ancient Jewish history! Or is there?

Firstly, the Old Testament has sometimes been described as the picture book of the New Testament. Here are three examples.

- In the story of the Flood (Genesis 6-8), the ark built by Noah was the one place of safety; and Peter draws a parallel between this and Jesus' sacrifice on the Cross (1 Peter 3.18-22).
- On the night before the Israelites came out of captivity in Egypt, they were told to kill and eat the Passover lamb and to sprinkle its blood on the door-frames of their houses: the blood would ensure that the people in the house would not suffer from the final plague that the Egyptians were about to suffer (Exodus 12.6-13). In the light of this we can better understand Paul's comment in 1 Corinthians 5.7 "For Christ, our Passover lamb, has been sacrificed" and John the Baptist's description of Jesus as "the Lamb of God, who takes away the sin of the world" (John 1.29).
- John 3.14-15 says "Just as Moses lifted up the snake in the desert, so the Son of Man must be lifted up, that everyone who believes in him may have eternal life". This makes little sense until we read the story of the plague of serpents in Numbers 21.8-9, with God telling Moses to set up a bronze snake on a pole: anyone who was bitten and looked at the bronze snake lived. Here, as in the other examples, we see just one way of being saved; and this points forward to Jesus as the unique way of salvation, or safety, in the New Testament.

Secondly, there is nothing in the New Testament quite like Psalms, Proverbs and Isaiah. Among many special books in the Old Testament these three stand out. The Psalms can help us to give expression to so many human emotions from joy and confidence to despair and anger. Proverbs contains much practical wisdom for day-to-day living. Isaiah contains some of the loftiest and most profound poetry ever written, as well as showing us God's character and loving purposes.

Thirdly, there are many special themes that come out with great clarity in the Old Testament books. Examples are God's tender love (see Hosea 11.1-9); or obedience to God's call – Isaiah did obey when he had a vision of the Lord (Isaiah 6), whereas Jonah at first disobeyed, with alarming consequences (Jonah 1); or a whole nation that gradually drifts from God, and the importance of having godly leaders: the books 1 and 2 Kings record a succession of good and bad kings and the effect they had on Judah and Israel.

Fourthly, the Old Testament offers special insights into subjects which are mentioned but perhaps not covered so extensively in the New Testament.

- Marriage: Genesis 1.26-28 and Genesis 2.20-24 set out God's blueprint for marriage; and Song of Songs celebrates the wonder of love and sexual attraction.
- Suffering: Job suffers undeserved calamities (Job 1 and 2), and the rest of the book is in dialogue form as he argues with God and with the friends who bring him misguided comfort.
- Bringing up children: Proverbs brings out the importance of training children – guiding them towards true wisdom (Proverbs 2.1-8) and away from such temptations as crime (1.10-19), adultery (5.1-20) and excessive consumption of alcohol (20.1 and 23.29-35).
- Foolishness: There is no book quite like Ecclesiastes, with its devastating portrayal of the follies of living for wine,

women, work and wealth (see especially chapter 2), and the closing words of wisdom in chapter 12 to "Remember your Creator in the days of your youth".

- The long haul: Few characters in the New Testament can be studied in depth over a long period of their lives. But it is quite different in the Old Testament. Abraham and Sarah longing for the promised child (Genesis12-21); Joseph hated and sold into slavery by his brothers but later rising to be Prime Minister of Egypt (Genesis 37-50); Moses born in Egypt, fleeing into exile but returning aged 80 to lead the Israelites out from captivity through the desert towards the Promised Land (Exodus 2 onwards, and see his lovely epitaph in Deuteronomy 34.10-12); David growing up as a shepherd boy and becoming the nation's most iconic king (1 Samuel 16-31) – these characters with all their strengths and flaws can be studied in detail over a large part of their lives; and they remind us that walking with God is more like a marathon than quick sprint.

Fifthly there are some very special people in the Old Testament from whom we can learn valuable lessons, some positive, some negative. Pharaoh kept hardening his heart and resisting Moses and therefore resisting God (Exodus 7-11). Ruth was a foreigner, but she was loyal and faithful in accompanying her mother-in-law back to Judah and eventually found joy and a new husband there (Ruth 1-4). Ahab and Jezebel, king and queen of Israel, based their lives on greed and godlessness and came to bad ends (1 Kings 16.29 onwards). Daniel was faithful to God in the seductive and hostile environment of exile in Babylon (Daniel 1-5). Nehemiah was far away in Susa and was cupbearer to the Persian king when God called him to the special task of rebuilding the walls of

Jerusalem after the exile (Nehemiah 1-6) – and how well he seized his opportunities and stuck to the task, despite much opposition!

For reading:

Proverbs 1.7 and Proverbs 1.20-33

For discussion:

a) Which books of the Old Testament do you feel you know fairly well or would like to know better?

b) What do you think are the most valuable sections of the Old Testament? Why?

c) Why might we regard the New Testament as incomplete without the Old Testament?

Confidence in the Value
of the New Testament

THE DATING AND HISTORICAL BACKGROUND: The 27 books of the New Testament were written probably between about 50 and 90AD, though these dates have been much discussed by scholars. Some would favour later dates, with the final books not written till well into the 2nd century. But the general backdrop is the Roman Empire. Judea was a small and not very important province of that Empire. The Jewish religion was officially tolerated, though not generally liked, by the Romans; and conversely the Roman occupiers were hated by the Jews. At first the Romans found it difficult to distinguish between Jews and Christians. So the Jewish problem smouldered on throughout the first century AD till it all came to a head with the Jewish War (66-70AD). Jerusalem was sacked by the Romans in 70, as Jesus in his final weeks of ministry had hinted would happen (see Matthew 24.1-28). This is such a cataclysmic event that it is hard to imagine the New Testament writers would have failed to mention it if it had already happened. They don't, which strengthens the case for supposing that most of the Gospels and Letters were written before the year 70. Meanwhile persecution of Christians as a separate group had begun in the reign of Nero after the fire of Rome in 64AD.

What is the New Testament: There are 27 separate books: the four Gospels recording the life, teaching and ministry of Jesus; Acts of the Apostles recording the birth of the Church and the spread of Christianity, particularly through Paul's journeys around the eastern Mediterranean; 21 letters written by Paul and other leaders to help various young groups of Christians; and Revelation describing John's vision of heaven and the ultimate triumph of God over the forces of evil. History (the Gospels and Acts), teaching (the letters) and prophecy (Revelation) – the pattern is similar to the three-fold division of the Old Testament into history, the wisdom books and the prophets.

Why was it written? The Apostle Peter talks about the importance of accurately preserving the record of the events upon which Christianity is founded. He is conscious that he and that first generation of disciples will not be around much longer (2 Peter 1.12-15), and that written records will become increasingly important. He implies that a collection of Paul's letters has already begun to circulate (2 Peter 3.15-16) – so the New Testament is beginning to take shape during his lifetime (and tradition says that he was martyred around 64AD). Peter is one of the original eye-witnesses, as he stresses in 2 Peter 1.16-18. John makes the same claim in his Gospel (John 21.24) and his first letter (1 John 1.1). Luke also mentions the importance of eye-witness testimony and claims to have investigated it all closely (Luke 1.1-4).

Many of the letters were written with specific purposes in mind. Examples are…

- Romans: Paul wrestles with how we can be justified before God, and where the Jews stand.

- 1 Corinthians: Paul deals with disunity and a case of immorality, and then answers specific questions they have raised – about marriage, about food offered to idols before being sold in the market-place, about his authority as an apostle, about spiritual gifts, about the resurrection of the dead and about collecting money for relief work.
- Galatians: Paul is combating legalism – those who claim we are saved by good works and keeping the Jewish Law, not by God's grace.
- 1 and 2 Timothy: Paul is guiding and encouraging the young Timothy, whom he has left in charge of the church in Ephesus.
- Hebrews: The (unknown) writer is explaining how Jesus's death on the cross is the culmination and fulfilment of all the Old Testament sacrifices.
- 1 John: John is combating the heresy of Gnosticism – the false view that we need a special form of knowledge to know God, to which only the initiates have access.
- Jude: Jude too is concerned about the infiltration of false teachers and the dangers they pose.

Finally we should note that Revelation was written in response to a specific command: "On the Lord's Day I was in the Spirit, and I heard behind me a loud voice like a trumpet, which said: Write on a scroll what you see and send it to the seven churches…" (Revelation 1.10-11)

What can we gain by reading the New Testament?

Firstly, and most obviously, it will help us to find faith. John near the end of his Gospel writes "Jesus did many other miraculous signs in the presence of his disciples, which are not recorded in this book. But these are written that you may believe that Jesus is the Christ, the Son of God, and that by believing you may have life in his name" (John 20.30-31). Luke has a similar aim, "so that you may know the certainty of the things you have been taught" (Luke 1.4).

Secondly, it will help us to know the Lord better. Reading the Bible is not just an academic exercise, not even just a study of the mind, the teaching and the character of Jesus. Paul wrote "I want to know Christ". Behind the human authors is the Divine Author, who speaks to us through his word.

Thirdly, we need to be challenged by the various characters in the pages of the New Testament, and not just the great and famous ones. Paul with his wonderful energy, vision, determination, loving care and endurance is a good starting point. But what about the faithfulness of 84-year-old Anna, who had been widowed quite young and devoted herself to prayer and worship? Or Timothy, who is a model for aspiring younger leaders? Or Barnabas, who certainly lived up to his name "Son of Encouragement"? Or Euodia and Syntyche, two ordinary women who were serving God at Philippi despite finding it hard to get on with each other? We have much to learn from these and many others. (See 2 Corinthians 1.8-11; Luke 2.36-39; 1 Timothy 1.18-20; Acts 9.26-27; Philippians 4.2-3.)

Fourthly, individuals and churches sometimes need guiding and correcting. As mentioned above, 1 Corinthians deals with a whole range of problems and gives relevant guidelines; and elsewhere Paul talks about all scripture being useful for teaching, rebuking, correcting and training (2 Timothy 3.16).

Fifthly, we need always to be ready to explain our faith to others, as Peter urges his readers (1 Peter 3.15); and very often the actual words of the New Testament have greater power and clarity than our own.

For reading:
2 Timothy 3.14-4.5

For discussion:
a) How well do you know the New Testament already, and what are your favourite books?

b) What would you say are the most important reasons for studying the New Testament?

c) How can we "always be prepared to give an answer to everyone who asks you to give the reason for the hope that you have" (1 Peter 3.15)?

26

Confidence in the
Face of Death

"**D**IE, MY DEAR DOCTOR, THAT's the last thing I shall do!" These are the last words attributed to Viscount Palmerston (1784-1865). And in more modern times Woody Allen said "I am not afraid of death, I just don't want to be there when it happens". Were they joking, or seeking to put off the inevitable, or trying to cover up what is a very natural fear?

Christian confidence in the face of death is well expressed by the poet John Donne (1573-1631):

> "Death be not proud, though some have called thee
> Mighty and dreadful, for thou art not so,
> For those whom thou think'st thou dost overthrow
> Die not, poor death, nor yet canst thou kill me...
> One short sleep past, we wake eternally,
> And death shall be no more; death, thou shalt die."

This confidence accords well with the words of Jesus to Martha at the grave of Lazarus: "I am the resurrection and the life. He who believes in me will live, even though he dies; and whoever lives and believes in me will never die. Do you believe this?" (John 11.25-26). It accords well with the dying words of Stephen the first Christian martyr: as the crowd stoned him he prayed "Lord Jesus, receive my spirit. Lord, do not hold this sin against them" (Acts 7.59-60). It accords well with Revelation 20.14: "Then death and Hades were thrown into the lake of fire. The lake of fire is the second death".

In the Old Testament belief in the after-life was only gradually developing. "It is not the dead who praise the Lord, those who go down to silence; it is we who extol the Lord, both now and for evermore" (Psalm 115.17-18). This passage paints a gloomy picture of death as a world of silence.

But sometimes the writers spoke better than they knew, as it were. "You will not abandon me to the grave, nor will you let your Holy One see decay. You have made known to me the path of life; you fill me with joy in your presence, with eternal pleasures at your right hand" (Psalm 16.10-11). This Psalm is attributed to King David. He may be referring here to the constant dangers through which God kept him safe when Saul was still alive and trying to capture and kill him. Or he may unconsciously be reaching out towards the idea of surviving beyond the grave and enjoying the eternal pleasures of heaven. The Apostle Peter preaching to the crowds on the Day of Pentecost applies this passage to Jesus: David died, he says, but he was giving a prophecy about Jesus, who was one of his descendants. Whatever David meant, it is quite clear that he could not face death with total confidence; he could not assert with all the clarity the New Testament writers display that death is not the end and that beyond the grave lies eternal life and eternal joy.

And this makes the confidence of the Old Testament character Job all the more remarkable. Job was a man who faced great calamities, losses and afflictions. Satan was permitted to attack his wealth, his family members and his health. Yet even when his wife said "Are you still holding on to your integrity? Curse

God and die!" he held on to his faith (Job 2.9-10). Later in the book, as he argues with his friends, he comes up with a wonderful expression of faith: "I know that my Redeemer lives, and that in the end he will stand upon the earth. And after my skin has been destroyed, yet in my flesh I will see God; I myself will see him with my own eyes – I and not another" (Job 19.25-27). Such a confident statement matches everything the New Testament has to say about death.

There is a but. Christians may well be confident about their eternal destiny; and yet the actual process of dying is fearful. To allay such fears, it would be wonderful to be taken straight up into heaven, like Enoch and Elijah (Genesis 5.24; 2 Kings 2.11-12), or to die in our sleep and know nothing of any painful process of dying. "One short sleep past, we wake eternally…".

Psalm 23 can be a real comfort. "The Lord is my shepherd" must be one of the most famous verses in the Bible. It talks of God as a shepherd who protects and guides his sheep; and that loving care extends right to the end of our lives: "Even though I walk through the valley of the shadow of death, I will fear no evil, for you are with me" (Psalm 23.4).

Others have found music helpful, and in particular the Matt Redman song "10,000 Reasons". It is heart-warming to read the story of Charlie, who was diagnosed with lung cancer that later spread to his spine, liver and brain. But all the way through his final days his faith remained strong as he sang or listened to that song.*

We need to pray for those who are near death; and for ourselves we need to find the Bible verses, the songs, the readings that will keep us close to God in the valley of the shadow of death.

For reading:
Philippians 1.19-26

For discussion:

a) Which passages of the Bible do you find the most helpful when thinking about death?

b) How can we prepare for death?

c) How can we best help others who are facing death?

---

* This is one of several such stories in the book "10,000 Reasons" by Matt Redman with Craig Borlase, published by David C Cook, 2016. See chapter 14 "Confidence in Worship" for other stories.

27

Confidence in the Trinity

ONCE SOME JEHOVAH'S WITNESSES CAME to our front door, and we had a long conversation. I tried to show them from the Bible that Jesus is God: they believe that he is just a prophet. My trump card, so I thought, was the passage where Thomas meets the risen Jesus, sees the marks of the nails and the spear and says "My Lord and my God!" (John 20.26-28). Their reply was "Oh, we don't know the answer to that one". This finally made it clear to me they were not going to acknowledge, on that day at least, that Jesus was God.

Many Christians struggle to understand the Trinity and are embarrassed when cynics ask them to explain it. God is one, and yet God is three persons. How can three be one, or one be three?

There are some well-known illustrations. Water appears in three quite distinct forms – ice, water and steam – and yet the chemical formula doesn't change. A clover stem has three leaves, even though it is one stem. An electric fire has power flowing through it; it produces a warm red glow in the immediate vicinity of the fire; and it spreads heat through a much wider area of the room. The power represents God the father; Jesus was God in visible form in one area of the world and for one comparatively short period; while the influence of the Holy Spirit has been spreading throughout the world ever since Jesus went back to heaven. But these illustrations can be misleading and only shed limited light on the problem.

Interestingly the word Trinity does not occur in the Bible, nor in Christian writings until Tertullian uses it towards the end of the second century AD; and it wasn't till the Councils of Nicaea and Constantinople in 325 and 381AD that the divinity of Jesus and of the Spirit and the doctrine of the Trinity were clearly affirmed. The four Gospel writers never broke off their narratives to discuss or try to prove God's triune nature. It is a doctrine that gradually developed in Christian thinking as the church struggled to make sense of Jesus and of the books of the New Testament. For those books had been written by the Apostles or by their close associates, and therefore had a special authority.

Judaism is a monotheistic religion, and yet there are hints of the Trinity in the Old Testament. In Genesis 1.1 the word *God* is plural but the verb *created* is singular; and then in verse 26 God says "Let us make men in our image, in our likeness". Isaiah 6.8 is similarly enigmatic: Isaiah hears the voice of the Lord saying "Whom shall I send? And who will go for us?" Then there is the figure of Wisdom in Proverbs 8: "I was there when he set the heavens in place, when he marked out the horizon on the face of the deep...Then I was the craftsman at his side. I was filled with delight day after day, rejoicing always in his presence, rejoicing in his whole world and delighting in mankind" (Proverbs 8.27, 30-31). It is hard not to think of Wisdom here in personal terms, especially when we compare this passage with John's Gospel, "In the beginning was the Word...Through him all things were made; without him nothing was made that has been made" (John 1.1, 3). We should also note how the Spirit comes to people in Old Testament times bringing wisdom or power. "Now Joshua son of Nun was filled with the spirit of wisdom because Moses had laid his hands on him" (Deuteronomy 34.9, and the NIV footnote gives Spirit with a capital S). Samson was confronted by a lion: "The Spirit of the Lord came upon him in power so that he tore the lion apart with his bare hands" (Judges 14.6). Samuel anointed David to be the new king, "and from that day on the Spirit of the Lord came upon David in power" (1 Samuel 16.13). Thus the Old Testament refers to God and the Spirit and a seemingly personal Wisdom figure, and the verbs give hints of the Trinity.

But we would know very little of the Trinity without the New Testament books. At the Last Supper Philip asked Jesus "Lord, show us the Father and that will be enough for us". The reply was "Don't you know me, Philip, even after I have been among you such a long time? Anyone who has seen me has seen the Father… Don't you believe that I am in the Father, and that the Father is in me?" (John 14.8-10). So the Father and the Son are, in some deep and unfathomable way, a unity.

Jesus shortly afterwards goes on to talk about the Spirit: "I will ask the Father, and he will give you another Counsellor to be with you for ever – the Spirit of truth. The world cannot accept him, because it neither sees him nor knows him. But you know him, for he lives with you and will be in you. I will not leave you as orphans; I will come to you" (John 14.16-18). Now, there are two Greek words meaning another: *heteros* means another of a different type, while *allos* (which is the word used here) means another of the same type. We have a friend at church who makes home-made wines. If he gives me a bottle and I later ask for another, I could be expressing dislike (another = heteros) or approval (another = allos)! Thus the Spirit is another Counsellor of the same type as Jesus. He is with the disciples at that moment, because Jesus is with them, and he will be in them when the Spirit comes down in power on the Day of Pentecost. When Jesus promised "I will come to you", he meant that he would come in the person of his Holy Spirit.

One of the disciples found all this puzzling, and Jesus gave a further explanation: "If anyone loves me, he will obey my teaching.

My Father will love him, and we will come to him and make our home with him" (John 14.22-23). *We* must refer to the Father and the Son, and they will come to each believer in the person of the Spirit.

Paul too points to the unity between God and Christ and the Spirit: "You, however, are controlled not by the sinful nature but by the Spirit, if the Spirit of God lives in you. And if anyone does not have the Spirit of Christ, he does not belong to Christ. But if Christ is in you…" (Romans 8.9-10). When he uses these interchangeable terms (Spirit, Spirit of God, Spirit of Christ, Christ), we can be confident that God is indeed three persons in one God.

There are very few verses of the Bible in which all three persons of the Trinity are mentioned. But in Ephesians 2.17-18 Paul is talking about the way Jesus broke down the division between Jew and Gentile: "He came and preached peace to you who were far away [the Gentiles] and peace to those who were near [the Jews]. For through him we both have access to the Father by one Spirit." Prayer is through Jesus, in his name; it is addressed to the Father; and it is with the aid and inspiration of the Spirit. Paul also gave us a lovely prayer of blessing at the close of 2 Corinthians: "May the grace of the Lord Jesus Christ, and the love of God, and the fellowship of the Holy Spirit be with you all".

For reading:
John 14.15-29

For discussion:
a) Does the Bible leave us with any other option that to believe in the Trinity?

b) Should we pray to the Father, or the Son, or the Spirit, or doesn't it matter?

c) How can we best explain the Trinity to non-believers?

28

Confidence in God's Unchanging Character

ISN'T THERE A BIG DIFFERENCE between the God of the Old and the New Testaments? In one he seems to be a God of anger and judgment, in the other a God of love. But then the New Testament claims "Jesus Christ is the same yesterday and today and for ever" (Hebrews 13.8), and Christians see the whole Bible as a unity. Where lies the truth? We will look at five aspects of God's character, and see that they occur in both parts of the Bible.

Anger: In the Old Testament God's anger was clear to see in such stories as the Flood, the destruction of Sodom and Gomorrah, the destruction of Jericho and the punishment of Achan (Genesis chapters 6-8, Genesis 19, Joshua 6 and Joshua 7). But in the New Testament too we see instances of his anger: Jesus drove the traders out of the Temple, Ananias and Sapphira were punished for their dishonesty, and God's wrath was poured out with the seven last plagues (John 2.13-16, Acts 5.1-10, Revelation 15.1).

Light: In the first chapter of the Old Testament God created light with the simple command "Let there be light" (Genesis 1.3). It must have been an amazing moment, when all that mysterious emptiness and darkness was suddenly filled to bursting with glorious light. Light carries all sorts of extra layers of meaning, including brightness, glory, purity and truth. The psalm-writer said "The Lord is my light and my salvation" and "The Lord God is a sun and shield", and one of the prophets wrote "Your eyes are too pure to look on evil" (Psalm 27.1; Psalm 84.11; Habakkuk 1.13). In the New Testament Jesus calls himself the light of the world (John 8.12); and in old age John wrote "God is light" (1 John 1.5).

Love: "God is love", says 1 John 4.8; and the Gospels are full of Jesus' love and care for the outcasts and the downtrodden in society. But the Old Testament too stresses God's love. God reveals his character to Moses in the words "The Lord, the Lord, the compassionate and gracious God, slow to anger, abounding in love and faithfulness, maintaining love to thousands, and forgiving wickedness, rebellion and sin" (Exodus 34.6). One of the shortest poems in the English language is this: "How odd of God to choose the Jews". Deuteronomy 7.7-8 explains why he did so - not because they were a large nation, but quite simply "it was because the Lord loved you". Psalm 136 says "His love endures for ever" 26 times in 26 verses. We also read of God's love in Lamentations 3.22-23 "Because of the Lord's great love we are not consumed, for his compassions never fail. They are new every morning; great is your faithfulness". The writer (Jeremiah according to tradition, though this is not totally certain) probably wrote these words just after his country had finally been conquered in 587 BC and he and most of his fellow Jews had been carted off to exile in Babylon. He was very conscious of God's loving care despite all the disasters that were happening to his nation: "For I know the plans I have for you, declares the Lord, plans to prosper you and not to harm you, plans to give you a hope and a future" (Jeremiah 29.11). God loves, and he never gives up on his people.

Spirit: A spirit is invisible: in the Old and New Testaments no one could see God physically unless God chose to reveal himself to their sight. The prophets Isaiah and Ezekiel saw visions of

God (Isaiah 6.1, Ezekiel 1.28). But Moses' request to see God's glory was only partially granted (Exodus 33.18-34.7). "Truly you are a God who hides himself" is the surprising assertion in Isaiah 45.15. So in Old Testament times, as well as in the years after the life of Jesus, people generally could only see God's work in the world, not actually see God himself. God's Spirit was active in creation (Genesis 1.2). God's Spirit came upon people and inspired them to prophesy - that is, to deliver his words - like Balaam (Numbers 24.2), Azariah (2 Chronicles 15.1) and Ezekiel (Ezekiel 11.24). God's Spirit also came upon people and inspired them to do mighty deeds - like Gideon (Judges 6.34) who won victories over the Midianites and other enemies, or Samson (Judges 13.25; 14.6; 15.14) who overpowered a lion with his bare hands and won victories over the Philistines. In the case of Saul, God's Spirit came on him when he was first anointed king and he started prophesying among a group of prophets, and then again early in his reign when enemies threatened the town of Jabesh Gilead and he went to their rescue (1 Samuel 10.10; 11.6). So the Israelites could not see God, yet they could certainly know that he was with them.

In the New Testament Jesus promised to send "another Counsellor to be with you for ever – the Spirit of truth" (John 14.16-17). The Spirit duly came down on the day of Pentecost, giving the disciples special gifts, inspiration and boldness. Again, they could see the effects of the Spirit but could not see God himself. "God is spirit", says John 4.24.

Fire: The writer of the letter to the Hebrews gives this warning, "God is a consuming fire" (Hebrews 12.29). In the Old Testament fire was the means by which God chose to reveal himself to Moses at the Burning Bush (Exodus 3.2-6). He led the Israelites out of Egypt and through the desert with fire by night and cloud by day (Exodus 40.36-38). He revealed his power when Elijah confronted the 450 prophets of the false god Baal by sending fire down to consume the sacrifice on the altar (1 Kings 18.22-38). But fire is a symbol, a metaphor. Fire can burn and destroy. Many times in Jewish history God punished the nation for drifting away from him - most notably when the Babylonians came and sacked Jerusalem and took most of the Jews off into exile. Both Old and New Testaments make it clear that we cannot trifle with God or treat his commandments lightly: we cannot play with fire.

Although human language fails to describe God fully and adequately, we find the same picture and the same characteristics of God presented in both the Old and the New Testament. This should not surprise us, for Jesus was the culmination of the Old Testament, and for a few years he bore the very image of the invisible God. He brought the Father into focus.

For reading:
Exodus 20.1-4; Malachi 3.6-7; Romans 11.22; Hebrews 13.8

For discussion:
a) Which parts of the Old Testament are most familiar to you, or is your picture of God based mainly on the New Testament?

b) What leads some people to claim that the God of the Old Testament is different from the God of the New Testament?

c) How might we answer them?

29

Confidence in Prayer

MANY PEOPLE WITH LITTLE OR no connection to the church have a vague feeling that prayer might be important and could just work sometimes. It has been said that there are no atheists in a lifeboat: we pray in a crisis, even if we don't pray at other times.

J.K.Rowling recently said on Twitter (8th October 2016) "If we all hit ctrl-alt-delete simultaneously and pray, perhaps we can force 2016 to reboot". And when David Beckham got injured before an important football match a few years ago, I recall a national newspaper inviting its readers to place their hands on an image of his foot and pray. On this occasion Uri Geller, who had a reputation for spoon-bending, called on the nation to unleash its healing powers. He is quoted as saying "I definitely believe in the power of healing, the power of prayer and the power of positive thinking. I can feel the energy".*

But vague feelings about prayer are not enough. Who are people praying to, and even if requests appear to be granted, where is the source of power? It would be dangerous to call on unknown and possibly malevolent powers. What does the New Testament teach about prayer?

The early church spent much time in prayer together after Jesus' ascension:

Acts 1.14: "They all joined together constantly in prayer", and those prayers certainly seem to have been answered in the outpouring of the Spirit and the preaching to the crowds in Acts 2.

Acts 4.24-31: Then there was opposition from the authorities. Peter and John were arrested, warned not to preach, and released. Immediately the believers prayed together, ending with the words "Now, Lord, consider their threats and enable your servants to speak your word with great boldness. Stretch out your hand to heal and perform miraculous signs and wonders through the name of your holy servant Jesus". The meeting place was shaken, they were filled with the Spirit and boldness, and the following chapters show how their prayers were answered.

Acts 10.1-5: Cornelius was a Roman centurion, but he was seeking God and prayed regularly. An angel brought him this message: "Your prayers and gifts to the poor have come up as a memorial offering before God. Now send men to Joppa to bring back a man named Simon who is called Peter." That led to Peter visiting him and explaining the Gospel to him and his household.

Acts 12.5: "So Peter was kept in prison, but the church was earnestly praying to God for him." These prayers were united, earnest, addressed to God, and specific – four important features of effective prayer. They had an immediate, miraculous answer, and very soon Peter was knocking at the door.

Acts 13.2-3: A group of believers at Antioch were worshipping the Lord and fasting. The Holy Spirit spoke to them about sending out Barnabas and Saul (soon to be called Paul) on a special journey. So again they fasted and prayed, commissioned them and sent them off on what was to be the first of several fruitful missionary journeys round the Mediterranean world.

Acts 16.25: Paul and Silas were in prison in Philippi in northern Greece. But they were not despondent. "About midnight Paul and Silas were praying and singing hymns to God, and the other prisoners were listening to them." Their prayers and worship were answered in another spectacular release from prison and the conversion of the jailer and his family.

Paul is known to us as a great traveller, preacher and writer of 13 of the 21 letters in the New Testament. We might forget that he was also a man who devoted a lot of time to prayer. In almost every letter he says he is praying for the recipients and giving thanks for them**. One example is "First, I thank my God through Jesus Christ for all of you, because your faith is being reported all over the world. God, whom I serve with my whole heart in preaching the gospel of his Son, is my witness how constantly I remember you in my prayers at all times, and I pray that now at last by God's will the way may be opened for me to come to you" (Romans 1.8-10). Sometimes he says he "makes mention" of them (1 Thessalonians 1.3 AV) – which might be quite a brief prayer, but the Greek word also has the lovely idea of reminding God of their existence. Sometimes he specifies in much greater detail what he is praying for them – strength, power, establishment in love and knowing the love of Christ (Ephesians 3.14-19). He must have had either a prayer list or a memory with a brilliant filing system. He prayed constantly and earnestly; and he was not put off by adverse circumstances.

So the Bible gives plenty of encouragements and examples of how to pray. But we don't find praying easy and are often asking questions like the following:

Should prayer be spoken or silent? At its simplest, prayer is talking with God, and the words can be spoken out loud or in our minds. We may move on later to wordless prayers and just holding situations or people up to him without using any words; indeed, we might be so overwhelmed by something that words are impossible. But Jesus gave us a pattern of prayer that consists of words.

Should prayer be formal or informal? The Lord's Prayer, which we shall examine in the next few chapters, is a good model prayer, covering the areas about which we should be praying. But in human relationships we don't constantly use formal, prepared statements, so it would be strange if we never used our own words when talking to God.

Should there be a pattern or should we pray as it comes? Sorry-thanks-please can be a useful pattern – confession, praise and thanksgiving, and requests. But patterns mustn't become routine to the point of boredom, and anyway each day brings new situations that need to be prayed over.

Should we use prayer lists or pray as things occur to us? The American evangelist D.L.Moody had a list of 100 people for whose conversion he prayed daily: 96 became Christians during his lifetime, and 4 at his funeral. That is an exacting challenge, but maybe a shorter list (of perhaps ten names) would be useful. One friend of mine prays alphabetically through a list of friends, starting again at A every few months and emailing them to ask for news and prayer requests. Lists stop us from forgetting important people and situations, but they must be revised at intervals and not become too mechanical.

Should we pray written or extempore prayers? This applies particularly to prayer meetings and church services. Either is fine. Some people lack the confidence to pray without preparation, others prefer spontaneity. The one essential is that the prayer should be humbly directed to God rather than proudly showing off to the people around us.

What should we pray about? Our own circumstances and problems, our family, friends, work, godchildren, our local church, Christian organisations we support, our government, our country, world peace…This is not an exhaustive list, and different people will be drawn to concentrate their prayers on different things. But prayer is a vital task. Paul talks about prayer in the context of the armour of God (Ephesians 6.10-18), and he was probably thinking of prayer when he wrote "The weapons we fight with are not the weapons of the world. On the contrary, they have divine power to demolish strongholds" (2 Corinthians 10.4). We are all on a "front line" with special opportunities to talk with friends or work colleagues and to share our faith with them.

What about prayers for healing? James 5.14-16 encourages us to pray for those who are ill, and there are some amazing stories in the Gospels and in the life of the church today of prayer for healing being answered. (We may not hear much about them: this follows the pattern of Jesus seeking to avoid unhelpful publicity, for example in Mark 1.43-44, Mark 5.43). We do need to acknowledge that not all prayers for healing receive the answer yes, and when disappointed we must humbly commit the situation to God. David Watson was a great Christian leader who died of cancer in 1984 despite many people around the world praying for him.

But God does often does give clear answers, maybe in quiet but loving ways, like the three people who came forward for prayer last week at the church I attend. One didn't think she should pray for herself, but she had breathing difficulties; one had a cough after some throat surgery; one had had a migraine for a long time; and all were healed. Another lady from the church had suffered from depression for most of her life. Several people had prayed for her, but it was through prayer at a church in Sheffield that she began to find healing. She also used to suffer from sinusitis and had facial pain whenever she had a cold. It went on for five years, and at last she gave up asking for prayer for this condition. But then she visited another church locally, asked for prayer, was healed and has had no recurrence of the pain for the last seventeen years.

For a final example I quote an email from a friend: "I suppose the most amazing healing miracle I've personally witnessed is in the life of a cockney friend of mine called Arthur, who went to be with the Lord a few years ago. But about 30 years before that he was healed of spondylosis. This is a painful condition of the spine resulting from the degeneration of the vertebral discs. Arthur used to be bent over and in constant pain and was only able to move slowly and laboriously. He was prayed for one day in the name of Jesus and he was instantly healed. Kathie and I are witnesses of the before and after. When I went to see him, he looked at me with a big grin and said "Watch this". Then he ran up and down the stairs of his house shouting "Look, I've been 'ealed, ve Lord Jesus 'as 'ealed me!" It made the hairs on the back of my neck stand on end."

What if our prayers seem to be unanswered? There are the obvious barriers to prayers being answered, like unconfessed sin (Psalm 66.18) or asking for purely selfish reasons (James 4.3) or not being persistent (Luke 18.1-8). Therefore keep going, keep trusting. A friend of mine was praying for someone who had been suffering pain for several months despite the prayers of many friends. He commented sympathetically "What us evangelicals often lack is an understanding of "mystery". Post-Reformation, it was as if we had the scriptures now, so could easily explain anything. We had "The Haynes Manual" of the Holy One. Mystery is not always a bad thing – just don't ask me to live with the outworking of it, such as in a long-term health issue like yours. It's always much easier to think of prayer as "cause and effect", but sadly, it does not seem to work like that. But it does not stop me from praying…".

The early church grew because it prayed. Paul's ministry was effective because he prayed. Prayer is a vital weapon in our spiritual warfare. Our churches and our own spiritual lives will grow if we pray.

For reading:
Matthew 7.7-12

For discussion:
a) What have you found to be most helpful in your own praying?

b) What happens if we, or our local church, fail to give time to prayer?

c) How do we make sense of those times when our prayers just seem to bounce back off the ceiling?

THE FASTING AND PRAYER
CONFERENCE INCLUDES MEALS

* www.dailymail.co.uk/news/article-109381/Nation-help-heal-Beckhams-foot-says-Uri

** Romans 1.8-10; 1 Corinthians 1.4; Ephesians 3.14-19; Philippians 1.3-6; Colossians 1.3-14; 1 Thessalonians 1. 2-3; 2 Thessalonians 1.11-12; 2 Timothy 1.3; Philemon 4

30

Confidence in the Lord's Prayer (1)

Our father in Heaven

Our Father in heaven,
Hallowed be your name,
Your kingdom come,
Your will be done, on earth as in heaven.
Give us today our daily bread.
Forgive us our sins
As we forgive those who sin against us.
Lead us not into temptation, but deliver us from evil.
For the kingdom, the power and the glory are yours now and
    for ever. Amen.

THE LORD'S PRAYER COMES IN slightly shorter versions in Matthew 6.9-13 and Luke 11.2-4; but the essence of it is the same, and it may well be that Jesus gave this model prayer to groups of disciples more than once. We shall look at it phrase by phrase, starting with "Our Father in heaven".

Right at the outset the prayer draws Christians together: the word *our* reminds us of our unity, the fact that we all belong to one family.

For some people *father* is a difficult word. But in the Old Testament a human father is portrayed as loving and protecting his children: "As a father has compassion on his children, so the Lord has compassion on those who fear him" (Psalm 103.13). A father is a figure of authority, love, blessing, teaching and guiding, and rescuing when the children are in trouble. For example…

- Isaac, the second of the three Patriarchs, near the end of his life blessed his sons Jacob and Esau (Genesis 27). A father's blessing was seen as important.
- Jacob was the head of a large family. He mourned many days when he received the (false) news that his son Joseph had been killed by a wild animal. He was the one giving the order to ten of his remaining sons to go down to Egypt for corn when there was famine in Canaan. His was the heart beating with anxiety for his youngest son Benjamin: his other sons had told him the Egyptian official insisted that their youngest brother must accompany them to Egypt on their next visit. And he was the one who sanctioned the decision for the whole family to move down to Egypt when he learned that Joseph was still alive and was in fact the Egyptian official (Genesis 37.33-35; 42.1-3; 43.1-14; 45.26-28).
- The priest Eli played the role of adoptive father when the young Samuel was brought to the House of the Lord to serve there; and when the Lord first called Samuel, Eli was the one who guided him as to how to respond (1 Samuel 3.1-10).
- Solomon (or whoever was the writer of Proverbs) in the early chapters of the book constantly stresses the importance of his teaching to his son. "Listen, my son, to your father's instruction…My son, if sinners entice you, do not give in to them…My son, do not forget my teaching…My son, pay attention to my wisdom…(Proverbs 1.8; 1.10; 3.1; 5.1).

In the New Testament Jesus reassured his listeners in the Sermon on the Mount, "Your Father knows what you need before you ask him" (Matthew 6.8). On another occasion he tells a parable about a father with two sons: when one goes off and wastes all his inheritance in profligate living, the father back at home never stops loving the boy and looking out to forgive and welcome him when he returns (Luke 15.11-32). Then in Romans Paul talks of how we can address God intimately as Father: "You received the Spirit of sonship. And by him we cry, *Abba, Father*" (Romans 8.15).

Someone once said that parents worry about their children: that's their job. If that is how an earthly father should be, God is even more loving and caring.

The phrase *in heaven* could make God seem remote. "God is in heaven and you are on earth, so let your words be few" says the author of Ecclesiastes 5.2. Alternatively it could reassure us that God is in the place of power, and this is the impression given by the visions of the Lord in Isaiah chapter 6 and Revelation chapter 1. The Creator of the universe is well able to hear our prayers and supply our needs. The amazing thing is that he invites us to have a relationship with him, a relationship based on his father-like love and our childlike trust.

For reading:
Matthew 6.5-15

For discussion:
a) How difficult is it to think of God as Father?
b) What do the words *in heaven* add to our understanding of God?
c) Should we use formal prayers, or pray using our own words, or both?

31

Confidence in the Lord's Prayer (2)

Hallowed be your name

T HE SECOND LINE IN THE Lord's Prayer, "Hallowed be your name", is perhaps the most difficult line of the prayer to understand. Part of the difficulty lies in the word "hallowed", not a word in every-day use. We also need to think about the significance of the words "be" and "name".

Firstly, *hallowed* means holy, honoured, revered; and holy means set apart, special. God is utterly different from us and greater than us; he is set apart, and so are the buildings dedicated to his worship. And yet, amazingly, Jesus said to his disciples "No longer do I call you servants...but I have called you friends..." (John 15.15 (RSV)). We need to approach God in prayer with the right blend of confidence and love and reverent awe.

Secondly, *be* can form part of a command, and many prayers are actually in the form of commands. They may be softened by adding the word "please". But how often have people prayed "Guide me in this situation", "Give me strength to cope with this problem" or "Heal my friend", and each time they have used the imperative form of the verb: they are giving commands to God - which seems strange! Yet Jesus' model prayer contains imperatives: "Give us...Forgive us...Deliver us...", so we are not being presumptuous in addressing commands to God. It's just that we must do so humbly, recognising our utter dependence on him.

Alternatively we could think of this phrase *hallowed be your name* as not quite a command but more like a wish. The expressions "May it be sunny tomorrow" or "May there be good news in the post today" are wishes. But whether it is a command or a wish, we could rewrite it like this: "May your name be holy".

Thirdly, why are we asking for God's *name* to be hallowed? The name of a person is very special; it is how we address them and get their attention. At a deeper level it is also how we think about them: a friend's name and their character and personality and memories of times we have spent in their company are all bound up together. [Therefore to use the name of God as a swear word is not only disrespectful and breaking the third commandment (Exodus 20.7), but it is also quite literally misusing the name – making a division between the mere name and God's great, loving, holy character.] We are praying that we, and others, may honour him, calling on him and depending on him in a way that is fitting.

The word "name" occurs frequently in the Bible. Here are just a few verses to ponder:

"Jerusalem, the city which the Lord had chosen...in which to put his name" (1 Kings 14.21). He wants Jerusalem to be particularly known as a city where he is honoured, a God-fearing city which acts as a beacon to the nations.

"The Lord answer you in the day of trouble! The name of the God of Jacob protect you...Some boast of chariots, and some of horses; but we boast of the name of the Lord our God" (Psalm 20.1, 7). "The name of the Lord is a strong tower" (Proverbs 18.10). If we are faced with a sudden danger and someone is standing some distance away, it is much easier to get their attention and help if we know their name. Similarly we can address God by name, calling on his help; and the best and most powerful thing we can do in a time of difficulty or crisis is pray to God.

"I am the Lord, that is my name; my glory I give to no other" (Isaiah 42.8 (RSV)). When Moses was called at the Burning Bush to go and lead the Israelites out of Egypt, he was worried that they would challenge him by asking God's name, and he wouldn't be able to answer. God's reply to Moses was "I AM WHO I AM" (Exodus 3.13-14). It's a name that reminds us that he exists from eternity, and for him all time is present. Much later Moses asked to see God's glory. God replied "I will cause all my goodness to pass in front of you, and I will proclaim my name, the LORD, in your presence. I will have mercy on whom I will have mercy, and I will have compassion on whom I will have compassion. But you cannot see my face, for no one may see me and live" (Exodus 33.18-20). Clearly God's name and character and glory are closely bound together.

"Fear not, for I have redeemed you; I have called you by name, you are mine" (Isaiah 43.1 (RSV)). "But rejoice that your names are written in heaven" (Luke 10.20). In the film "Love Actually" Sam was bowled over when he discovered that Joanna, the girl he worshipped from afar, knew his name! How much greater a privilege is it that our names are known to God and that they are recorded in heaven!

For reading:
Isaiah 43.1-7; Philippians 2.5-11

For discussion:
a) Do these two passages help us to understand God's character better?

b) Should we approach God as Holy Creator and Lord or as a friend? Or is it possible to use both approaches simultaneously?

c) What makes us fearful, and how might Isaiah 43.1 help us to cope?

32

Confidence in the Lord's Prayer (3)

<u>Your Kingdom Come</u>

KINGDOM MEANS KINGLY POWER, OR the area where that power and authority is exercised. What a difference it would make if the whole world bowed to God's kingship and acknowledged his authority! No more war, greed, crime, oppression, hatred, terrorism, kidnapping or even minor acts of unkindness, cold-shouldering and lack of love...But the world is full of these things, as we know from TV, newspapers and our own observation. The problems are far too great for us to solve by ourselves, but we can pray "Your kingdom come" and draw on a power infinitely greater than our own.

A 19th century hymn provides a good commentary on this clause from the Lord's Prayer:

> Thy Kingdom come, O God,
> Thy rule, O Christ, begin;
> Break with thine iron rod
> The tyrannies of sin.

(It's a hymn in the form of a prayer. We are asking God that his kingdom should come into a world bound and fettered by sin. But his kingdom will not come till the end of the world and the second coming of Christ – a time also referred to in the next three verses.)

> Where is thy reign of peace,
> And purity and love?
> When shall all hatred cease,
> As in the realms above?

(There is at least some peace, purity and love in the world. But, unlike the situation in heaven, God's kingdom has nothing like 100% control over men's hearts, which are full of impurity, hatred and war.)

> When comes the promised time
> That war shall be no more –
> Oppression, lust and crime
> Shall flee thy face before?

(We long for an end to war, oppression, lust and crime, but we know only God's rule can eradicate evil.)

> We pray Thee, Lord, arise,
> And come in thy great might;
> Revive our longing eyes,
> Which languish for Thy sight.

(So why doesn't God break in? Come on! Surely he is powerful enough to zap evil and let good take over! We long for that, and are wearied by all the evil we see around us! And this is the mystery of evil - the freewill that God has given, allowing mankind to obey or disobey him.)

> Men scorn Thy sacred Name,
> And wolves devour Thy fold;
> By many deeds of shame
> We learn that love grows cold.

(People misuse God's name as a swear word, and ridicule Jesus' followers for their faith. Sadly there are some "wolves in sheep's clothing" in the Church itself; but most sad of all, even some seemingly committed members of the Church lose their love for God.)

> O'er heathen lands afar
> Thick darkness broodeth yet;
> Arise, O Morning Star,
> Arise, and never set.

(This was written in Victorian England - supposedly a Christian country sending out missionaries to the distant nations who needed the light of the Gospel. And they still do need that light. But so do we, in a country which has increasingly drifted from any Christian roots it might have had in the days of Aidan, Cuthbert, Oswald and later that fine Christian King Alfred the Great.)

For reading:
Matthew 3.1-12

For discussion:

a) If this prayer is answered in major and visible ways, what difference might it make in our country, our society, our government.

b) How do we react to falling church attendance figures and surveys suggesting that two out of five Britons are uncertain whether Jesus actually lived?

c) What signs of love for God growing cold should we beware of in ourselves and in those close to us?

33

Confidence in the Lord's Prayer (4)

Your will be done, on earth as in heaven.

O H IF ONLY...HEAVEN IS SO utterly perfect: why can't earth be like that too?

We get glimpses of heaven in Isaiah chapter 6: "I saw the Lord seated on a throne, high and exalted...Above him were seraphs...And they were calling to one another: "Holy, holy, holy is the Lord Almighty"...and the temple was filled with smoke". In Revelation chapters 4 and 5 the Apostle John gives us a similar picture of the divine throne surrounded by people praising the Lord; and then in chapters 21-22 he describes the glory and joy of the new heaven and the new earth - no more death or mourning or thirst or impurity or darkness.

Meanwhile back on earth in our newspapers and on TV we have floods, shootings, bombs, crime, terror, hatred, the very opposite of that vision of heavenly glory and peace. It is a stark contrast.

So do we wring our hands in despair? Or do we indulge in a life of selfishness, pleasure and maybe even breaking the law, working on the principle "If you can't beat 'em, join 'em"? Or do we try to do something about it, doing acts of kindness and seeking to make a difference in at least one tiny corner of this suffering world? Or do we pray? After all, someone once said "When we work, we work. When we pray, God works". That person was Hudson Taylor (1732-1805), founder of the China Inland Mission, and one who certainly put this dictum into practice: he used to rise daily at 5am in order to read the Bible and pray.

We need to work AND pray. Paul writes "Continue to work out your salvation with fear and trembling, for it is God who works in you to will and to act according to his good purpose" (Philippians 2.12-13).

If we don't pray, we may rush around in our own strength and pride. But we haven't asked for God's wisdom and guidance, we may be pursuing wrong or unhelpful courses of action, and we only have our own inadequate strength to achieve our goals.

On the other hand if we don't act, we are likely to be so heavenly minded as to be of no earthly use, and there is the danger of laziness and a proud spirituality. There are times when, in a sense, we can be the answer to our own prayers. A vicar was once visiting a town three miles from his home, walking down the High Street past the grand but failing church, and praying that the Lord would send someone to be the new minister there. Then he clearly heard God's voice saying "It's you"; and that was for him the start of a remarkably fruitful ministry there.

Take Saint Cuthbert. He spent some years as a monk and then as a hermit in private prayer and meditation on the Farne Islands, but in the last few years of his life God called him to much more active service as a Bishop in Northumbria. He sets us a good pattern of prayer combined with work.

So let us pray for God's will to be done in our homes, in our families, in our locality, in our country, in Europe and all over the world. It's an ever-widening circle. But it starts with ourselves, as we align our will with God's will. For there are only two groups of people in the world: those who humbly say to God "Your will be done", and those to whom in the end God says (very reluctantly and sadly) "Your will be done".

For reading:
Revelation 21.1-5

For discussion:
a) Paul had a real struggle between doing his own will and doing God's will (see Romans 7.15-25). How far have we got in coping with that struggle?
b) What are the important things to pray for as we long for God's will to be done on earth?
c) How can we find a better balance in our own lives between work and prayer?

34

Confidence in the Lord's Prayer (5)

Give us today our daily bread

FOR THOSE WITH A GOOD income, a large freezer and easy access to a supermarket, it is hard to pray this sentence of the Lord's Prayer with any sense of urgency! We might even switch off for a moment, or feel a bit smug. Yes, I know there are some war zones in the world where they really need to pray this prayer; yes, I know I must put a real effort into saying "Your will be done" and "Forgive us our sins". But this bit...I'm all right here...no need to worry.

Deuteronomy 8.18 is a powerful antidote to this attitude: "Remember the Lord your God, for it is he who gives you the ability to produce wealth". How did we come by that income to buy food and other necessities? God gave us our abilities and job opportunities, and we should probably pay our debt of thanks to him more often than we do.

Daniel 5.23 is another verse that hit me between the eyes when I first read it. Belshazzar King of Babylon has been showing off his wealth at a little soirée (just the one thousand guests!) when some writing appears on the wall. Only Daniel can understand what it says and what it means. Belshazzar's kingdom is about to be destroyed, and Daniel goes on to explain the reason: "But you did not honour the God who holds in his hand your life and all your ways". A different translation is even more dramatic: "But the God in whose hand is your breath, and whose are all your ways, you have not honoured" (Daniel 5.23 RSV). Our life, along with our every breath, is utterly dependent on God's sustaining goodness, love and care. He has given us our life, our health and strength to get to the shops, and a whole host of people to provide the food that is available there - farmers, harvesters, packers, transporters, food standards officers, store managers, checkout staff...not to mention a peaceful country and police to deter holdups and robberies in supermarkets. It's all so much more complicated than it was for the Israelites in Exodus wandering in the desert and receiving daily supplies of manna and quails; or those 1st century AD shepherds, fishermen, innkeepers and others for whom financial security was a distant dream and daily bread a real struggle.

Another insight is found in Proverbs 30.8-9: "Give me neither poverty nor riches, but give me only my daily bread. Otherwise, I may have too much and disown you...Or I may become poor and steal, and so dishonour the name of my God". Gluttony and drunkenness are both condemned frequently in the Bible. Praying for daily bread and giving thanks before meals will help us guard against these dangers.

Most sobering of all is a parable that Jesus told about a rich fool. After a particularly good harvest he decided to build bigger barns to store all his goods and then to sit back, eat, drink and be merry. Little did he know his life would end that very night, and that he had been neglecting God while he stored up wealth for himself (Luke 12.16-21).

We need to thank God for his provision, and remember those who lack the daily necessities. We may be called to help them in particular ways, whether by giving money or by more direct action. There are those who help run food banks, which are a lifeline for some households; while other people have a passion for avoiding waste, rescuing food that shops would otherwise throw away and then cooking free meals for those in need.

Robert Burns sums it up most memorably:

> "Some hae meat and canna eat,
> And some wad eat that want it,
> But we hae meat and we can eat,
> And sae the Lord be thankit."

For reading:
Luke 12.13-34

For discussion:
a)   Have we been too complacent about our daily bread?
b)   Study the three Old Testament passages quoted above (Deuteronomy 8.18; Daniel 5.23; Proverbs 30.8-9): what thoughts particularly stand out for you?
c)   How should we respond to those in our own country and abroad who lack their daily bread?

35

Confidence in the Lord's Prayer (6)

Forgive us our sins

ALONG TIME AGO AT A Sunday lunch table far far away (I was brought up in the suburbs of London) we had a particularly delicious plum tart and custard. Afterwards, as some of the tart still remained, my young fingers strayed towards a plum. I was told very firmly not to touch it; but I did, and was soundly rebuked and sent to my room. I felt miserable; I had disobeyed my parents, and, temporarily at least, I was estranged from them. Eventually I came down, said sorry, and all was well again.

Why does the Lord's Prayer include the clause "Forgive us our sins"? Here are some FAQs.

1. **I'm a pretty decent sort of person, aren't I? Why should I be praying for forgiveness?** Jesus told a story about a man who ran up to him and asked how he could inherit eternal life, having kept all the commandments from childhood - or so he thought. He found the answer very hard to take: "Go, sell everything you have and give to the poor, and you will have treasure in heaven. Then come, follow me" (see Mark

10.17-23). Jesus had put his finger on at least one area of the man's life which wasn't perfect: he was clinging to his wealth. So with us: who can claim to be totally perfect? A few seconds thinking about the first and greatest commandment to love God with all our heart, soul, strength and mind should be sufficient to show us that we all fail and all need God's forgiveness. Or take the Ten Commandments: which of us can honestly say we have kept every single one of them - never stolen so much as a paper clip, never lied, never abused God's name, never misused Sunday, God's special day?

2. **What is sin? What is a sin? And are these questions identical?** Sin is described in various ways in the Bible, for example transgression, falling short, or iniquity. We transgress God's laws when we break his commandments. We fall short (a metaphor from archery) when we miss the mark, the target of God's perfect standards. And iniquity means a natural bias towards going our own way and doing or saying or thinking wrong things: we find it hard to stick to the straight and narrow path. Sin is the state we are all in by nature; a sin is just one particular instance of our doing wrong.

3. **What happens if we don't confess?** Firstly, we cannot know God at all unless we start by admitting our sinfulness to him. There has been a great gulf between God and us ever since that first act of disobedience described in Genesis chapter 3. Jesus bridges the gap and offers us forgiveness; but we need to ask him for that forgiveness - he will not force it on us, even though he longs for every sinner to turn back to him. So we are unforgiven sinners until we confess.

Secondly, we may well experience what the writer of Psalm 32 felt: "Blessed is he whose transgressions are forgiven...When I kept silent, my bones wasted away through my groaning all day long". We may feel awful when we are conscious of our guilt, as I did over the plum. But even if we don't feel that guilt, we are nevertheless guilty.

4. **How can we be forgiven?** It is on the basis of Jesus' death in our place on the cross. Jesus came to earth not just to preach and teach but, most important of all, to give his life as a ransom for us (see Mark 10.45). As a famous hymn puts it,

> He died that we might be forgiven,
> He died to make us good,
> That we might go at last to heaven
> Saved by his precious blood.

5. **Why do we confess so often?** There was a great emphasis on confession in the Church of England's 1662 Communion Service and in Morning and Evening Prayer. Today we tend to use more modern language, and perhaps (though not necessarily) we have lost the intensity of sentences like "We have erred, and strayed from thy ways like lost sheep. We have followed too much the devices and desires of our own heart. We have offended against thy holy laws...But thou, O Lord, have mercy upon us, miserable offenders". The fact is that even as Christians we sin, we fail again and again, and we are constantly in need of forgiveness. Jesus was probably illustrating this when he washed the feet of the disciples at the Last Supper: "A person who has had a bath needs only to wash his feet" (see John 13.10). Walking in the streets makes the feet dusty: walking through life, even when we are already Jesus' followers, we will frequently sin. We will not need to start the Christian life all over again from square one, we will not need to be adopted once more into God's family, but we will often need to pray "Forgive us our sins".

For reading:
Psalm 32.1-7

For discussion:

a) As we read this Psalm, do the feelings of the writer sound familiar to us?

b) How can we best help those who think they live decent lives and don't need God's forgiveness?

c) Read Isaiah 53.3-6. Reflect on how closely this passage describes Jesus' death on the cross, even though it was written about 700 years earlier.

36

Confidence in the Lord's Prayer (7)

As we forgive those who sin against us

A LONG TIME AGO I HEARD two stories about forgiveness which have stuck in my memory: I hope I have remembered the details correctly. One is associated with the bombing of Coventry Cathedral in November 1940. Afterwards people were praying the Lord's Prayer in the ruins, but they got stuck at the words "as we forgive those...". Then someone led the way, and they prayed that hard phrase.

The other story concerns two schoolboys. One bullied the other mercilessly; but many years later, after a career in the church and rising to be a bishop, he was approaching death and even so long afterwards felt very bad about what he had done. So he wrote to the other person, who was now a judge, asking for forgiveness. The judge agonised over the letter; eventually he wrote back "Very sorry, cannot forgive".

Jesus told a story about a servant who owed his master a vast sum of money. The master called him to account, he had no means of paying, he begged for mercy and time to pay off the debt - and the master took pity on him and let him off completely! But then that servant met a fellow servant who owed him a very small sum.

Did he show mercy, just as mercy had been shown to him? No way! He attacked him and threw him into jail, insisting that the debt should be repaid. The master was very sad and angry to hear this, and he reinstated the vast debt of the first servant. Jesus ended the story with the words "This is how my heavenly Father will treat you unless you forgive your brother from your heart" (Matthew 18.23-35).

If we are conscious that God has forgiven us so much that was wrong in our lives, the least we can do is to forgive others. In fact, this story teaches that our being forgiven is conditional on our forgiving others.

There is another motive for forgiving others, and that is the effect it has on us if we don't forgive. The New Testament talks of "a bitter root" growing up inside us (Hebrews 12.15). Forgiving can be a source of strength and liberation; holding on to a grudge has the opposite effect.

Gordon Wilson was a peace campaigner in Northern Ireland. In 1987 he was injured and his daughter killed in the Enniskillen bombing; but a few hours later he was able to say in a BBC interview "I bear no ill will. I bear no grudge."

What can we do if we feel we could never say those words in similar circumstances?

- We can pray specifically about this issue. God understands us better than we understand ourselves. Psalm 139.2-4 says "You perceive my thoughts from afar...Before a word is on my tongue you know it completely, O Lord", and Hebrews 4.15 describes Jesus as a high priest who is able to sympathise with our weaknesses.
- We can analyse our feelings to see whether there is some underlying cause, which might possibly be easier to deal with first.

- We can look at the example of Jesus, his patient suffering (1 Peter 2.21-24) and his forgiveness for those who when they crucified him drove nails through his hands and feet.

For reading:
Matthew 18.21-35

For discussion:

a) What thoughts strike you from this passage in Matthew 18?

b) Is it enough to say "I forgive that person, but I can never forget what they did"?

c) What should we do if we realise we are in the habit of holding grudges?

37

Confidence in the
Lord's Prayer (8)

Lead us not into temptation, but deliver us from evil

"I COULDN'T HELP IT. I CAN resist everything except temptation." Oscar Wilde had a wonderful way of putting things! But what exactly is temptation, and what does this sentence from the Lord's Prayer mean?

In the Greek text the word translated *temptation* also means *testing*, and the final phrase could be neuter (*evil*) or masculine (*the evil one*). Having said that, the words are still not easy to explain, even though we may have said them hundreds of times!

God doesn't tempt us: James 1.13 makes this clear. We might say that he tests us to build us up, while Satan tempts us to bring us down. The Old Testament book Job backs this up. In this poem with its extended dialogue about suffering, God permits Satan to afflict Job and so test his faith (see chapters 1 and 2). Temptation in itself is not sin. All human beings are tempted: it is sin only when we give in to the temptation to do something we know in our heart of hearts is wrong.

It is helpful to look at some different translations.

- "Do not bring us to hard testing, but keep us safe from the Evil One" (in the Good News Bible.)

- "Do not let us be put to the ultimate test", says one commentary*, and it compares this passage to Matthew 24.22 where Jesus promises that the coming days of great trial and tribulation will be shortened for the sake of his followers. (It is pretty certain that this passage refers to the Jewish War and the Romans besieging Jerusalem about 40 years later in 70 AD.)
- "Lead us not into temptation [leaving us there to be overwhelmed], but deliver us out of the evil [to which it would seek to lead us]" is Guy King's expansion of the passage**. He says we should not be praying for an easy Christian life, but we should be praying out of a sense of our own weakness. And we should remember 1 Corinthians 10.13: "No temptation has seized you except what is common to man. And God is faithful; he will not let you be tempted beyond what you can bear". Everyone is tempted. Everyone suffers. God knows, understands, and helps.
- "Do not allow us so to be led into temptation that it overwhelms us, but rescue us from the evil one", writes John Stott***: he reminds us that the Devil is strong, we are weak, and our Father will deliver us if we call on him. That echoes Psalm 50.15, one of my favourite verses: "Call upon me in the day of trouble; I will deliver you, and you will honour me".

So we should certainly pray for the strength to resist the temptations that will inevitably come. We should recognise that our only hope in the face of attacks from the world, the flesh and the devil is to trust in the Lord and draw on his strength. But we can also be part of the answer to our own prayers. Don't put ourselves in temptation's way (like the boy who had been forbidden by his parents to swim in the local river, but he took his swimming trunks with him anyway, just in case he was tempted). "Flee the evil desires of youth, and pursue righteousness, faith, love and peace..." writes Paul in 2 Timothy 2.22. And Oscar Wilde was wrong when he said "The only way to get rid of a temptation is to yield to it".

For reading:
1 Peter 5.6-11; James 1.12-15

For discussion:
a) What thoughts strike you from these two passages in the letters of 1 Peter and James?
b) What do you think is the best way of expressing the meaning of "Lead us not into temptation, but deliver us from evil"?
c) Do you sometimes feel that your temptations and sufferings are unique and quite unlike anyone else's? If so, how does 1 Corinthians 10.13 help?

---

*   The New Bible Commentary Revised, ed. D.Guthrie and others (IVP 1970) page 825
**   Guy King: New Order (Marshall, Morgan and Scott 1943) page 78
*** John Stott: Christian Counter-culture(IVP 1978) page 150

38

Confidence in the Lord's Prayer (9)

For the kingdom, the power and the glory are yours, now and for ever. Amen

T HIS DOXOLOGY IS NOT PART of the original text of Matthew's version of the Lord's Prayer, so presumably it was added later because it was used in the worship of the early church. My dictionary defines doxology as "a liturgical formula of praise to God", and it is certainly appropriate that this great model prayer should end with such a peal of praise.

The kingdom, the power and the glory - it is easy to let these words pass our lips without really thinking how great our God is. The words refer to three different aspects of God's character and being.

- He is King - "King of Kings and Lord of Lords", as Handel's *Messiah* puts it so eloquently.
- His power is shown in the creation of this vast universe, as well as in his acts of minute daily care and intervention in the world.
- And one day we shall see his glory, a glory that only a privileged few have seen during their lifetime - men like Moses, Isaiah, Ezekiel and John the author of Revelation.

What happens when we first turn to Christ? It makes no difference whether it's a slow journey of developing faith or more like Paul's Damascus road experience. We change kingdoms: we move from Satan's realm to God's lordship. A friend of mine used to raise a glass of wine with the toast "To the King in Heaven" - a nice reminder of our true King.

This talk of a kingdom implies that the earth is a battle ground, which is exactly what it is. So much of what we see and hear going on in the world confirms that the forces of evil are strong, and the kingdom of darkness reigns in many hearts. "For our struggle is not against flesh and blood, but against the rulers, against the authorities, against the powers of this dark world and against the spiritual forces of evil in the heavenly realms", writes Paul in Ephesians 6.12. The good news is that God's power is far greater. Jesus destroyed the powers of sin and death and the devil through his death on the cross. We are on the winning side, and ultimately that victory will become clear and visible.

And the glory? One day we shall see that glory. We love pictures of the Royal Family or the interior of Buckingham Palace, and the fortunate few go there to receive an OBE or a Duke of Edinburgh award. What grandeur, what riches, what glory! But Heaven will be infinitely more glorious. Human language struggles to describe that glory: note how many times John uses similes with the words *as* and *like* in Revelation 1.12-16.

Moreover God is eternal. He is from everlasting to everlasting. He is the great I AM. Philip Pulman in one of his novels portrays God as old, weak, tired and ready to die: nothing could be further from the truth! He is alive, he reigns and will reign for ever. As for us, eternal life starts now in our relationship with God while we are on earth, and it continues into God's eternity in the New Heaven and the New Earth. This is the truth, even though the concept is breath-taking and more than our minds can fully grasp.

It's fitting to finish with Amen, a Hebrew word meaning "So be it", an emphatic "YES!".

For reading:
Exodus 33.18-34.9; Isaiah 6.1-8; Revelation 1.12-16

For discussion:
a) What thoughts strike you from these passages in Exodus, Isaiah and Revelation?

b) How do the words kingdom, power and glory help us in understanding God better?

c) Evil is so strong in the world (as we are reminded in Ephesians 6.10-13). Why do you think that is, and what should we do about it?

39

Confidence that it's not too late

THERE'S A STORY ABOUT A man in prison who was given a copy of the New Testament by an organisation called the Gideons. He was a smoker. He had some tobacco, and was using the Bible's thin pages to make cigarettes; but at least he read the pages before he smoked them. In due course he came to John 3.16, probably the most famous verse in the Bible; and the words "God so loved the world..." really hit home. They helped him to come to faith in Jesus (and to give up smoking!).

At the end of that chapter comes a statement that is in a way even more startling, John 3.36: "Whoever believes in the Son has eternal life, but whoever rejects the Son will not see life, for God's wrath remains on him."

This sentence divides the whole of the human race into two camps, those who believe in Jesus and those who reject him. There is no middle group: it is a simple choice - eternal life or eternal death. So what does the verse mean, where do we stand, and what do we have to do?

What is eternal life? It starts now and means knowing we can be with God for evermore, both here on earth and after death. We will be part of the new heaven and the new earth described in Revelation chapters 21-22, in a place which is more wonderful and more glorious than anything we could possibly imagine.

<u>**What is the alternative to eternal life?**</u> It is being cut off from God for ever. It is choosing hell rather than heaven - and whatever else it is, Jesus made it clear that hell is a place of torment, regret and separation from everything that is good.

<u>**How do we obtain eternal life?**</u> By believing in Jesus; and that means much more than vaguely thinking that he exists. It means entrusting our lives to him, confessing our wrongdoing to him, obeying him and living in the sunshine of his presence from now on.

<u>**But I've never really rejected him, have I?**</u> The Greek phrase translated *rejects* really means *does not obey*; and we have all been guilty of going our own way, living for self and not obeying his commands.

<u>**Why is God angry?**</u> Because of sin - our natural inclination to break his rules and to live in a self-centred way. We may think we are pretty decent people, and the world in general may have that same view of us; but we don't live up to his standards, and we need his forgiveness. So in that sense we have rejected him.

<u>**So if that is what the verse means, where do we stand right now?**</u> If we believe (and go on believing - it is what is called the continuous present tense in the original Greek text), we already have eternal life and have nothing to fear when death comes. The only alternative is that we reject him (and go on rejecting him) till the day comes when we *will* not see life. That is the future tense: there *will* come a time when it will be too late.

But right now that leaves the door slightly open. We may be beginning to be convinced that the reality of heaven and eternal life is wonderful, that the alternative of being cut off from God for ever is awful, and that we haven't yet started believing in Jesus. If that is what we are thinking, then it's not too late to act - to pray a very simple prayer like "Jesus, I believe in you. Please forgive all the wrong things I have done, and please come into my life from now on". Prayer is simply talking to God - don't let anyone convince you that it has to be more complicated than that! And those words, sincerely meant, will take us from the second half of the verse to the first - from eternal death to eternal life. The dying thief who was crucified alongside Jesus was given the most amazing eleventh hour opportunity: all he managed to say was "Jesus, remember me when you come into your kingdom", and it changed his eternal destiny (Luke 23.42-43).

People delay and make excuses. Our excuses may be the product of complacency and laziness: "I'm all right as I am", or "I just couldn't be bothered". Or we may have big philosophical or intellectual questions like "How can you believe in an uncreated God?", or "What about all the suffering and evil in the world?", or "Why are there so many other religions?". Or it may be moral problems, or hangups that are buried in our sub-consciousness - "I don't want to give up my independence, my occult involvement, my porn addiction, my gambling, my alcohol abuse". Whatever the cause of the delay, we need to think it through and then stop making excuses and putting off the vital decision. Maybe John 3.36 will jolt us out of excuse mode and help us to see that *today* is the day to forget the excuses and make a new start.

Because, right now, it's not too late.

For reading:
John 3.16-21; John 3.36; Isaiah 55.1-9

For discussion:
a) What excuses do people we know make for not becoming Christians?
b) It may be unfashionable to talk about the wrath of God, but what does it mean, and is it important?
c) Is it ever too late to find God?

40

Confident Faith

URING MY FIRST WEEK AT university many clubs and
societies were eagerly trying to attract new members. One
was a Christian organisation which described itself as "for
those who are seeking and for those who think they have found".
That sounds rather vague and uncertain. Were they trying not to
sound arrogant, or did they genuinely believe that we can't really
be sure we have found the truth, the gospel, the good news about
Jesus, the secret of eternal life?

In the Old Testament Job speaks in a very different tone: "I
know that my Redeemer lives" (Job 19.25). If he was less sure, he
might have said he wished, or hoped, or suspected, or thought it
very probable; but he said "I know".

Similarly in the New Testament Paul writes "I am not
ashamed, because I know whom I have believed, and am convinced
that he is able to guard what I have entrusted to him for that
day" (2 Timothy 1.12). Was Paul so confident? The answer must
be yes; for he endured so much suffering in the course of his
travelling and preaching. He describes some of his hardships in
2 Corinthians 11.23-33. He was frequently in prison, frequently
flogged, frequently shipwrecked; he was stoned (but survived), he
was sometimes deprived of sleep, food and drink, and he was often
in danger from robbers or false friends. Would he have endured

all that if he wasn't totally sure of the Lord he was serving? Again we hear the words ringing out "I know".

Jesus himself talked of this certainty. "Now this is eternal life: that they know you, the only true God, and Jesus Christ, whom you have sent" (John 17.3 RSV). He also said "If you continue in my word, you are truly my disciples, and you will know the truth, and the truth will make you free" (John 8.31-32 RSV). Christianity is a relationship with a person – a person who we know is there and who we encounter in his word, the Bible.

We need to foster that knowledge and help it to grow. Peter's second letter is largely on this theme. He starts by urging his readers to grow in faith, knowledge and love; he talks of the importance and reliability of the scriptures; and his closing encouragement is "Grow in the grace and knowledge of our Lord and Saviour Jesus Christ" (2 Peter 3.18). Studying God's word is fundamental to this process. The American preacher D.L.Moody (1837-1899) said "So few grow, because so few study"; and the British preacher C.H.Spurgeon (1834-1892) said "A Bible that's falling apart usually belongs to someone who isn't".

So where does faith come in? Hebrews 11 is a chapter surveying the faith of a whole range of characters from the Old Testament; and it starts "Now faith is being sure of what we hope for and certain of what we do not see" (Hebrews 11.1). They were certain of what they believed. They knew. And they acted on their faith. Noah built the ark – it must have seemed a pretty stupid thing to do, until the rains started. Abraham left his home and travelled to the promised land – a leap into the dark, trusting God's call. Moses had been brought up in all the luxury of the royal household in Egypt – he rejected it all and chose to side with God's people.

The story continued into New Testament times and beyond. Peter and John spoke boldly when threatened by the Jewish authorities: "We cannot help speaking about what we have seen and heard" (Acts 4.20). Stephen was stoned to death for his boldness in speaking of Jesus, but he kept praying right up till the moment of his death (Acts 7.59-60). Paul was obedient to the promptings of the Spirit even though he knew that prison, hardships and death awaited him. He was certain that completing the tasks laid on him by the Lord was far more important than his personal safety (Acts 20.21-24).

One book of the Bible that lays much stress on knowing God is the letter 1 John. It seems that John wrote this letter to combat the false teachings of Gnosticism – the belief that you need special enlightenment or knowledge (*gnosis* in Greek) to escape from the evil material world. By contrast John claims that he has seen and touched the Word of life, Jesus, and that he is the one through whom we gain eternal life and have a relationship with God the Father (1 John 1.1-4). He goes on to make some important statements on the theme of knowing.

"We know that we have come to know him if we obey his commands…If anyone obeys his word, God's love is truly made complete in him. This is how we know we are in him: whoever claims to live in him must walk as Jesus did." "But you have an anointing from the Holy One, and all of you know the truth. I do not write to you because you do not know the truth, but because you do know it and because no lie comes from the truth." "But you know that he appeared so that he might take away our sins." "We know that we have passed from death to life, because we love the brothers. Anyone who does not love remains in death." "And this is how we know that he lives in us: we know it by the Spirit he gave us." "I write these things to you who believe in the name of the Son of God so that you may know that you have eternal life." "We know that we are children of God, and that the whole world in under the control of the evil one. We know also that the Son of God has come and has given us understanding, so that we may know him who is true. And we are in him who is true – even in his Son Jesus Christ. He is the true God and eternal life."*

John keeps stressing the word *know*. We know facts ("we know that we have passed from death to life…we know that he lives in us…we know that we are children of God"). But we also know a person ("we have come to know him…so that we may know him who is true").

Obedience, living like Jesus, having a special anointing or empowering from God, knowing that he takes away sins, loving our fellow believers, having his Spirit living in us, believing in Jesus' name – these are the hallmarks of the Christian and the basis for Christian certainty.

For reading:
1 John 5.13-21

For discussion:
a) How much do you sympathise with people who say we can't know God and eternal life?
b) How does faith relate to knowledge?
c) What has helped you to grow in faith and knowledge?

---

*   1 John 2.3-6; 2.20-21; 3.5; 3.14; 3.24; 5.13; 5.19-20

Also by the Author

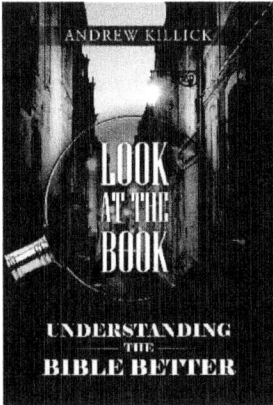

Look at the Book
Understanding the Bible Better
ISBN 978-0-9567187-9-2

So you are sitting there on the pub quiz team, and they announce a round on the Bible. How well would you fare?

This book is for those who would like to get to know the Bible better – and not just for the sake of pub quizzes.

Why should we study the Bible?

Jesus said at the end of the Sermon on the Mount (Matthew chapters 5-7) that anyone who hears his words and obeys them has foundations in life – like a house built on a rock; but anyone who hears them and doesn't put them into practice is like a house built on sand. We need foundations in life – especially when things go wrong – things like health, job, relationships.

There are 66 books in the Bible. The aim of this book is to get to know the books and build those foundations of understanding.

Through 24 chapters, twelve chapters each on the Old and the New Testaments, street lamps will be installed at regular intervals in order to light up the whole street, and your knowledge of the Bible will grow.

Suitable for those with a desire to know more about the Bible in smaller doses, chapters can be read in any order, with helpful hints included throughout. At the end of each chapter there is suggested reading for those who haven't the time to read the whole of the book under discussion.

*It's lively, accessible and inviting. I enjoy the variety of presentation and am very impressed with all the Helpful Hints and the Appendix [giving very brief summaries of every book in the Bible]. I do hope many get to know of it. – **The Rt Rev John Pritchard, Former Bishop of Oxford***

Lightning Source UK Ltd.
Milton Keynes UK
UKOW05f0328090317
296221UK00001B/31/P

9 780995 530720